# YOUR
# INNER
# COUNCIL

*Connect with your inner voice & intuition to*
*create personal success in life and business*

*Stacy Nelson*

# YOUR
# INNER
# COUNCIL

*Connect with your inner voice & intuition to
create personal success in life and business*

BADASS PUBLISHING CO · CALIFORNIA

Creative Development Editor: Heather Doyle Fraser
Copyeditor: Donna Higton
Designer: Danielle Baird

ISBN-13: 978-0-692-52886-0
ISBN-10: 0-692-52886-5

First Edition

BadAss Publishing Co. — Temecula, CA
www.BadAssPublishingCo.com

**I AM GRATEFUL** for so many people who inspired and supported this work. My family, my friends, my coaches, my colleagues, my clients. Each person who touched my life touched this book somehow.

My fear is that by listing you out individually I will forget someone critical...so instead I'll be calling you, messaging you, telling you that I am so extremely thankful for having you in my life.

And yes, I thank my Inner and Outer Councils for the connection, the insights, and for generally kicking my ass until I hit publish.

DOWNLOAD THE

# COMPANION WORKBOOK

FOR FREE AT

www.YourInnerCouncil.com

# All great leaders take council.

# introduction

Advisors, boards, councils...we get that image. To run a powerful business, having a panel of experts on your side is key. Sitting in a board room in session working out the details of x-y-z, everyone giving their unique perspectives from the divisions they run. Ultimately it's the Chairman's or President's or Empress of the Universe's responsibility to take the input into consideration and make a plan of attack.

And that all makes sense because we can't be an expert in all things right?

How great would it be to have access to the most powerful beings, the greatest minds and spiritual leaders ever known, to be able to sit in council with them daily and get guidance and input that would ultimately be up to you to implement?

# What if you already had that?

What if you already have a council and you just didn't know it? Enlightened advisors who give you multiple options so you can decide your next steps...

Building our businesses and our lives...THESE ARE INTERNAL JOBS.

Each of us has access to amazing knowledge and inspiration every single day and to our very own Inner Council.

Our Council is an absolute connection with Source, and with the TRUEST voices of YOU. It's our power and our magic sitting there waiting to be asked for assistance. This isn't something outside of yourself, it's IN YOU. Sitting with your Inner Council is like having a relationship beyond measurable value.

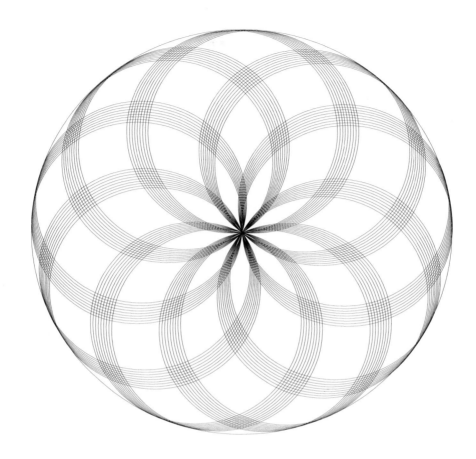

My journey began with

Nine circles...

Nine seats...

Nine warriors...sitting in council, each an aspect of myself.

As we sat, I saw their strengths in my life. I sat in the center of them all—in the tenth seat—and turned to hear each one's voice.

Each of these guides that live inside of me.

The challenge of writing this book wasn't intellectual, it was more challenging to dismiss the intellectual side of me. It required me to dive into self expansion. I had to lean into the Spiritual Warriors who sit in my Council and together we learned to trust and love my inner voice more.

The unity of myself with the wholeness of source—that's the good stuff.

That's the **BIG GOAL**...

To be able to use all the aspects of myself that hold my gifts and talents and turn the dial up in my business, my relationships, my life. That's awesomeness.

Inside each and every one of us is a direct link to Source, God, The Universe, Spirit—whatever you want to call it. I will call it many things...replace my words with whatever words feel good to you.

These members of my Council are the parts of myself that I lean on. ALL powerfully direct me and my vision. When I'm feeling constricted, they inform me and when I'm expanding they support me.

They are not definitions.
They are not containers meant to pigeonhole me or any of us into a type.
They are also not beings outside of myself.

They are in me and around me, waiting for me to tap into their wisdom.

I can embody all of them or none of them at any given time. Feed them, and I grow and thrive. Starve them, and I feel lost and alone.

They are the expression of my highest self, and they hold my stories, my blocks, and my super powers. They reflect in perfect harmony my own expansion and contraction.

Their voices resonate as my own. Their mission is precise and loving.

We each have Inner Councils waiting to engage in powerful conversations.

This is where we're going because Your Council is in session right now. The more you get to know each of them intimately, to know what they each need to fully expand the more you will learn to trust and rely on your own inner voice.

Everything we need to live the most beautiful life, to create love and freedom and inspiration and just general awesomeness is available in this board room inside of us, the wisest of the Universe sitting there waiting for you to ask them to help.

Join me. Take your seat. Meet your Inner Council.

*I am a Warrior, a Priestess, a Goddess.*

*I am powerful, beautiful & whole*

*I hear doubts and fears, but I know that they do not serve me*

*and I set them aside.*

*In battle, I cannot be distracted by weakness or anything less than love and FULL*

*presence, confidence, and knowingness.*

*I am patient.*

*Rushing in means defeat.*

*Watching. Observing.*

*Waiting for the right moment to strike.*

*Allowing events to unfold around me and intuitively knowing when to move,*

*instinctively responding to what is being created.*

*And by pausing, observing with all of my senses,*

*I become the true essence of a Warrior Priestess,*

*changing that which is against me, and molding the world into beauty...created*

*by the magic that flows around me and through me.*

*I am a Warrior, a Priestess, a Goddess,*

*intimate in the fierceness of what it means to be a woman and*

*the beauty of what it means to mold the magical force of life itself.*

*I am a Warrior, a Priestess, and a Goddess.*

*Powerful.*

*Beautiful.*

*Whole.*

When I first wrote these words I was lying in the dirt—literally on a pile of dirt, in my jammies, dust gradually covering my fingers and toes until they were ashen, the smell of fresh soil that only morning brings hanging around me, wafts of fragrant flowers coming from the grapefruit groves.

I was on the brink of a breakthrough, and my whole world was rocking—literally rocking. Like a weeble-wobble, I felt as if I were very grounded at the base but the further up my body I went the more I rocked like a boat, to and fro.

So I asked for advice.

My friend Allison messaged me 'go lie in the dirt and allow the sun to charge you and see what comes to you.' So I got up out of bed and abandoned my morning coffee to cool on the nightstand. (You know I was desperate if I left my coffee untouched.) Out I marched onto my property, dogs looking at me questioningly.

The pile of dirt 50 yards out looked about right. I settled into it like an arm chair and attempted to meditate. The sun warmed me through my whole body, the rays piercing through my eyelids, greeting me with morning grace. Little flecks of the broken granite and clay wiggled between my toes and fingers, finding their way down the back of my neck.

"Meditate damn-it!" I say to myself. Breathing, trying to release the spins, I realized that it wasn't working—why did I think this would work?

Resigned to the fact that a deeper state was eluding me, I sighed. Still rock-ing and now filthy, I opened my eyes and sat up. There at my feet was a rock shaped like an arrowhead. Being a bit of a natural rock hound I instinctively picked it up. A smile crept onto my face, for holding that rock I felt balance for the first time in a days.

In my head I heard, "this is a path of a warrior, are you ready to be the Warrior Priestess you have always been?"

I stood up feeling grounded and powerful and marched myself right back inside and into my bathroom (I wasn't getting back into bed with dirt all over me...) I wrote that poem, "I am a Warrior Priestess."

Then I hopped in the shower and I heard the doubt in my mind...WTF is a Warrior Priestess and who the hell would want to read about that? It's like woo-woo to the max, and I certainly can't show that stuff. And furthermore I've never been into the whole warrior thing, let alone Goddesses and Priestesses. This is something I know nothing about. What would make me write something so lame?

And the spins came back.

And this time they were even stronger. I held onto the wall in my shower to make sure I didn't fall over, feeling like I had been here before—wobbling at the edge of change.

Opening and closing the door on myself. I was expanding into a new version of me—that next level. Once that previous self started to diminish and I leaned into that more connected space inside of me—well, that sense of self wasn't there any longer. So if I wasn't that and I'm not fully connected, where am I?

Wobbling.

And then I heard "When the energy comes through, allow it to come through." It is uncomfortable to restrict the flow of energy...Do I want to play full out and be open or do I want to control the flow...opening only between the hours of 12 and 2 when it's convenient?

My energy was bottlenecking.

And the more I expanded, the more apparent it became that I no longer needed to control the process. But this is what I had been doing for so long. Controlling the process to keep me normal and safe.

# DON'T BE WEIRD

I remember as a child I was painfully shy, preferring to watch rather than interact or speak. I was always happy on my own, free to read or create mansions for my Barbies out of paper and cardboard and any other small items I found around the house. I had this area in my room between my bookshelf and my dresser where I would squeeze in and sit as small as I could so that I could read without anyone finding me, happy in what appeared to be my isolation.

I never felt alone. I was never in doubt that I had a cosmic support system. People may have scared the shit out of me but my guides were always there to protect me.

I just had this fear of telling anyone that they existed.

I was weird. Quiet. Empathic. I had guides who told me when to turn left for the best spot and what book to go grab. What I mostly learned growing up was that the only way I could fit in was to not talk about any of it, even to myself.

As an adult I dove into self development, surely there was a socially acceptable way to be a more whole person, right? I had many aha's. I bought an inordinate amount of books and took classes. I meditated and said things like 'I don't want to sound too woo-woo but' and occasionally threw out a snazzy Law of Attraction term. I studied all of the world's religions and read tons and tons and tons. I felt stuck and small.

I wondered what my bigger destiny would be. How to live a more authentic life.

But at the same time I wasn't really truly digging deeply.

Because I kept stopping at the point between Shelf-Help and 'This will make me weird again,' and I just wanted to be accepted. I was suppressing my abilities, my higher self.

The interesting thing is, even though I never trusted my own inner wisdom, I always had huge trust in what I called my guides. My guides were always with me, guiding me, protecting me, making sure I never wanted for anything. Even times in my life when I should have been in desperate need, I wasn't. I always wondered why my life always felt easy, even the times that would have crippled others—being assaulted in high school, losing my beloved grandparents in college, having my first child at 22 as a single mom. I never felt completely alone—misunderstood and not always with the outward signs of having friends—but never alone or on my own.

My guides were always there taking care of me and giving me everything I truly needed.

I'd hear messages and I'd follow in complete trust, knowing that it couldn't be wrong because it came from beings outside of me who cared for and loved me without boundaries. They were like my own Fairy Godmothers, creating an all too easy life.

And then I heard the message...it's time to write our book.

# MY WARRIOR CAME OUT

I was tired of looking normal and being quiet. I had to put my big girl pant-ies on and write this book, the one that most scares me. The one that col-lapsed me in the shower and makes my heart palpitate when I speak of it. The one that pushes me past my comfort zone.

This time felt like something outside of me calling. Must be my guides right?

I imagined myself sitting down, pen in hand, automatic writing, channeling the voices in my head down onto the white space on the page. I practiced each and every day for weeks. What came out was pages and pages of illegible scribble. Literally—scribbles, like an earthquake monitor on a fault line. Sometimes the writing would be long and flat and sometimes the let-ters would take up half of the page height up and down, up and down. I could hear the words but my body was having spasms the second the pen hit the page.

So, I hired a Spiritual Mentor. As a coach myself I have hired many business coaches, so I know how powerful a coaching relationship can be. I figured that I needed to be able to better communicate with this 'other' source so I could get the book done. I needed training.

My mentor is a Channel as well and I have experienced her powerful med-itations many times in the past. I figured that she would be the best person to help me deepen my channeling abilities, to help me get past my spiritual blocks so I could embrace the parts of me I had set aside.

And, in truth, my mentor was the best person to help me, but I was wrong about one thing—thinking it was something or someone outside of me who would be doing the writing.

See, the work we did together wasn't to allow me to hear my guides better, but to lift the separation I felt from them. There was them and there was me. And I was little and small and they were oh so wise and powerful. It was easy to trust and believe what they said. If it came from me, well that gave lots of room for judgment didn't it?

So 'their' book would be awesome. Mine would be...questionable.

What we worked on was a shift in perspective. In order to truly bring forth something that was in alignment with me and source, I had to understand that I am always connected with source. In fact, the voices I've always heard, the intuitive nudges I receive, the words and images that flash through me, the empathic chills I get when a miracle occurs...it was nothing outside of me that created all of that.

It was ME tapping into the expanded version of myself, swimming in that ocean of universal super juice. Our inner voices are messages from the divine...we are not separate from them.

There is no singular 'I'. 'I' do not write anything, 'I' do not create anything and 'I' am never alone in action.

The most beautiful things come from a deeper source.

They come from a place where 'WE' write, and 'WE' create. 'WE' is where we finally understand that we are all connected.

Settling in, taking a deep breath and connecting—to my inner voice.

I have seen it time and time again...when my clients start trusting the voice of their intuition their worlds start opening up. They live with more confidence and peace. Calmness.

As I registered all of this and began to integrate it into my being, I started to recognize my guides as my Inner Council, aspects of myself that show up in every situation. Those voices that tell me to turn left or to call someone; they are merely the connected pieces of me speaking in a voice loud enough for me to pay attention. It's not something bigger or better than me, it is a bigger and better version of me.

**You see, each one of us is connected. Our guides and our intuition, our Angels or our Guardians, each of these beings are connected by the never ending, never separate source. I have come to understand that our most powerful insights and transformations come when we are plugged into that universal energy flow.**

I also understand that each of us has the flow going through and around us all of the time, and that at a deeper level, we can interpret and communicate within the flow. We can drink directly from the cosmic super juice, and our Inner Council—at its very best—is our direct line to the juiciest juice.

This is the book that inspired me, even before I wrote it, before I knew my Council in such detail. It is a book of introduction and beginnings and becomings, and it is sacred to me.

No more wobbling.

I know personally how powerful life becomes when we claim our own Inner Councils. It is our right and privilege to connect with ourselves and tap into the wisdom all around us to create whatever we choose to create.

And I am thankful that you are here with me, to walk this path together. Have fun, linger, play, cry, feel the words reverberate in your heart.

Dig your toes into the dirt, and allow your coffee to grow cold. And when you are ready, Your Council wants to have a word or two with you...

# THE NINE

Our Inner Council consists of Nine main aspects. This number is sacred around the world and I'm sure I could add some nine-y stuff, numerology, chanting...just a paragraph or a few lines because I 'should' to enrich the experience for some. But really it doesn't matter, because the Nine aren't part of a rigid personality-typing or a way of identifying you in the world.

The Nine aren't abstract entities outside of you either. They are aspects of your own highest self.

They are ALL inside of you, always. The more we all develop and cultivate the beauty and strength each of them bring to the table, the more complete and beautiful our lives and businesses become.

Each of the Nine is equally important in different ways. We can call on the strength of one or the softness of another depending on what is most needed in our life. We demonstrate different levels of expansion with each of them every day. We can embody their bigness or we can lessen ourselves and become the starved and needy version of each aspect. They inform each other of imbalances and support each other all of the time.

Our Inner Council is always loving, and I feel that love when I take the time to connect with them—with ME. There is no separation, just a feeling of being perfectly at peace...at home.

The aspects of my NINE each represent someone who has dedicated themselves to a craft, to a way of being. Someone who is focused and will fight for a cause.

**That cause is me.**

We have full access to our own unique Inner Council inside of us at all times. Let's meet them...

**A WORD OF CAUTION**...don't use this book as another reason to compartmentalize yourself more.

Compartmentalizing ourselves comes up in conversations a lot with me (who the hell do I hang out with that this would be a normal conversation?). It's amazing how much we all divide ourselves into 'appropriate' roles, buttoning up to show our 'good' side, the side that will be accepted and liked, right?

My first session with my spiritual coach revealed something I was all too familiar with—the many faces of Stacy. There was football/tennis mom Stacy, wife Stacy, entrepreneur Stacy, coach Stacy, mother Stacy, daughter Stacy, a whole bunch of others and then at the very end hidden behind everyone else there was spiritual woo-woo Stacy.

I learned very early in life that this last side wasn't one to be worn loudly; that most people don't approve of guide-seeing, aura-reading, thought-reading, emotion-feeling little girls. It made me weird in school. More to the point, having gone to psychic fairs as a young girl experiencing the barrage of energy in the room and what I perceived as a child as those weird, weird, freaky weird people made me want it even less. I shoved her back in the recesses of my mind and only let her out with a sacred few who knew me well, like my Grandma and my mom. They educated this spiritual side of me, reading books and talking privately about new revelations and learning. But still, spiritual woo-woo Stacy remained a silent partner in my life.

As I got older, the pain of being hidden became too great, so I started letting her out more and more. She was still separate however, as if I could control when and where I could be spiritual.

My work with my coach helped me to lessen my control...to allow her not just to come out, but to weave her way through each of my different aspects, to be just as comfortable talking about Source at a rugby match as in a session. It took practice, but the more I let her out the harder it became to control her; to keep her separate from the rest.

Compartmentalizing ME was no longer an option. I still have control issues...it's still a work in progress, as I lean into the next level of expansion, and that first step was to show up as a unified front, whole and strong as one person rather than fragments of self.

So how can you integrate who you are more? How can you bring your whole self to the table each and every time? Where are you controlling your own flow to show up as perfect? How can you release control?

Use these Council Members to create a whole, unified YOU.

# CREATOR

— AND —

# STARTER

Life is a grand experiment
where we get to create things from nothing

# 1

# *the first seat*

You know the Big Bang Theory...where practically everything was created from nothing? Our Inner Creator lives it, breathes it, probably caused it. Fearlessly rushing forward into the unknown and having fun starting new things. The Creator isn't about drawing pretty pictures or just about creativity or art (although that does feed it); it's the piece of us that is capable of starting businesses from nothing but an idea, or writing a book from a concept that appears one day in the shower, rocking you to the core.

Every business on the planet was launched by someone with a strong Inner Creator. Imagine a world without entrepreneurs and you'd have a world disconnected from their Inner Starters. The light bulb was created by a Starter. The telegraph, smoke signals, sliced bread...that spark of something from nothing and the drive to see if it can be real? That's the domain of the Inner Creator.

# THE WORLD **NEEDS** US TO **START**, TO **CREATE**.

We need people who will lead the way, who will experiment and try new things. The world needs us to lean into this vibration more and more. I encounter clients everyday who have hidden their Creator behind their fears; who are unwilling or unable to take those first magical steps; who are so focused on a viable outcome that they don't get involved in the grand experiment.

## THE UNKNOWN IS THE MOST POTENT FUEL FOR THE CREATOR TO EMBRACE.

It doesn't mean there is no fear, it's just that the tingle of fear is a sign of stretching into something new. It's the excitement of starting on a new adventure, hoping that you packed appropriately and trusting that you can buy more supplies if you need them.

**When we lean fully into our Creator,** we find the place where we don't just create to create, but we create only the things that we deeply connect with...that feel right. And we allow ourselves to choose a few things to create instead of frantically doing them all, or conversely doing none.

**When we are repressing our Inner Creator,** we become unwilling to take the first step and then we get stuck. We become unable to choose.

**When we don't trust the capability of the Creator,** we just keep getting ideas. And when we only focus on the ideas and not the implementation, we get overwhelmed and backlogged.

**When the creative fires are set too low,** we lose our natural moving state of freedom and we feel the need to fight for everything. Obstinate and unmoving, we hide behind a fierce or even a detached facade to hide our insecurities and feelings of inadequacy. For me that means I become all force and no flow.

I personally need to constantly fuel my Creator by giving myself outlets to create. When I don't do this I become stuck, I don't innovate, and I stagnate. Some days I do it by writing, or doodling or making jewelry. Some days it's by creating a new client or creating a new program for my business.

**When our creative fires are lit up on HIGH,** we understand that dabbling isn't powerful. A creator doesn't just have great ideas. A BALANCED Creator puts those ideas into action. A developed and MASTERFUL Creator also knows that flow is the most important part of creating powerfully, and when you are in the flow, there is no room for force.

# S L O W I N G  D O W N

the pace of our Inner Creator and keeping it in balance with the natural ebb and flow of the Universe is key. When we nurture this aspect regularly, there isn't as much pressure to do. The fear of missing out on doing something isn't an issue because we can trust that we will only start the things we are most meant to start.

# FLOW VS. FORCE:

## CAN YOU LET YOUR INNER CREATOR OUT?

I will **MAKE** this happen by myself.

It was my battle cry. Like an author forcing herself to write gibberish in the "designated time", or an artist painting just anything so the walls will be filled, or the actor pretending they do not have the flu so the show will go on.

I will **MAKE** this happen.

Even if by forcing, what is produced is less than awesome or inspiring, it will happen. It becomes a creation of the mind, knowing that it must be done at all costs.

I will **MAKE** my business work.

I will **MAKE** my body be just so.

I will **MAKE** my life conform.

All **force**, no *flow*.

When I first started on the coaching path I led with that force energy...I had a posting schedule with themes mapped out. Perfect launch and marketing schedules in place. I was going to MAKE this business that was calling to me from my heart and soul. Years of internet and in-person marketing experience behind me, I took the plunge.

At the end of the year I had grossed $1,150.

Every plan I had made failed. All my graphs and flow charts and schedules and excel spreadsheets were useless. I threw spaghetti ideas out into the world in a desperate hope that ONE of them would stick.

I carried on.

# I WOULD **MAKE** MYSELF SUCCEED.

I got even more clever in how I was forcing things along. I started caring less and less about the product while my ego had meltdowns in the background.

Bruised and battered, my Inner Creator started looking for new things to create that weren't just about building my business. My mind and my Creator were in constant battle, coming up with clever plans to MAKE business versus going with the flow of my creation.

Until one day when I literally took every spreadsheet and task list and the cute little color coded "things to do" I had on my wall, and threw them all in the trash.

*I started reclaiming my day.*
*I started doing less.*

I bought myself a bunch of markers and—in an art journal—started to create for no reason during business hours. I remember those first few pages filled with guilty thoughts like, "I'm glad no one is here to see me coloring while I'm supposed to be working on my business." I started writing for no reason. I started posting the things I wrote from my heart instead of the slick marketing copy.

## *I started doing things that were against the 'rules' of business.*

I showed up in videos without pre-scripted messages. I threw out my business cards. I started making jewelry in between coaching sessions.

The more I created the less force I felt. It became easier and easier for me to feel like I was in FLOW. I was feeding my Creator. I wasn't inhibiting her and laying down the laws of proper creation. I was allowing her to show up as herself.

Without the separation of flow and business an amazing thing started to happen...The Creator stepped in and helped to CREATE clients from a soul-filled place. No logic or planning, just connected creation. My business started growing. In fact the less I did the more I created.

*I got support in areas that didn't feel creative and allowed myself to be the artist of my life.*

## I DECIDED TO BUILD A MASTERPIECE.

My business as a coach is an art form...never taking the same shape twice, each artist has her own style, her own color preference and medium. The coach creates her own unique brushstrokes on the souls of her clients. It's an expression of our inner selves and who we are and what we bring to the table. Creating paradigm shifts for others requires us to be fully present and fully authentically our own powerful selves.

Up to the point when I threw out all of the spreadsheets and task lists, I had been sitting in a room painting by numbers, copying from someone else's canvas, doing the things I was told I needed to do to MAKE a business. But I wanted to create art.

Art requires passion and dedication and an overwhelming willingness to break every single rule to make a masterpiece. Art required me to pick up that brush over and over again to really be able to feel and smell and see the paint in my dreams. To have it embroiled in my essence.

My business became beautifully crafted, sometimes one color at a time, sometimes by splashing all the colors on the canvas and rolling around in it. It's an art form, a great form of expression and emotion.

Where would we be **TODAY** if we had allowed our Starter to create yesterday?

I threw away the paint-by-numbers crap and started creating my business like I would a masterpiece.

My Inner Creator **had** to be let out in order to create my powerful successful practice. There was no other way for me...I had to step into the FLOW of creation and out of the mental FORCE of business rules.

Each time I feel stuck or frustrated in my business, I recognize that I have repressed my natural creative energy.

## *No creativity = no clients.*

No desire to start anything (conversations, programs, etc.), no fuel in my creative tank.

Always be creating in unexpected ways.

Pick up the pen and paper and write, or paint, or make something fabulous to eat. Explore the ways your creative juices are fed and allow them to flow all over the place.

**LET YOUR INNER CREATOR OUT!**

# STARTING VS. FINISHING

On paper, I make NO sense.

I am a serial entrepreneur. I get ideas and instantly think 'how can I monetize that?' It was always enough for me just to get things going. But people don't understand that. In fact I found out early in life that people who start stuff are misunderstood. We're called flakes and unfocused.

We live in a society where *finishing* what you start is far more treasured than *starting* anything.

- Finish your dinner

- Finish your homework

- Finish your sentence

- Finish school

- Finish whatever it is you've started so you have something solid to show for it

We are a results driven society. We very rarely hear about the scientist who works on experiments for a lifetime only to show no solid results. In fact, that scientist isn't a very likely candidate for grants or funding simply because there's no clear output, no defined return on investment. We simply don't care about existential questioning that doesn't have an answer or formula for us to categorize and compartmentalize. We want solid responses and results. We celebrate the scientist who finds a neat ending to his experiment and wraps it all up into a pill to deliver to the world.

Honestly, I've never really been that scientist.

My Inner Creator is strong. She loves to follow inspiration, even when it doesn't make logical sense. When I willingly start new things simply because I can, when I create things from nothing—when I am a STARTER, the independent leader inside of me screams 'I will not follow convention' or sometimes even logic. When I allow that vibration to take over I become a powerful doer, paving a path through the unknown, leading the way.

Sometimes I feel nothing but sadness and regret that I couldn't just be "normal."

Until I realized that the strongest part of me is simply underused in most people. That my Creator is in fact a superhero.

The shame I always felt around being multi-passionate and starting one adventure after the next changed in that moment. I felt as if I finally saw the divinity and perfection of who I was as someone who starts shit. That perhaps I would be misunderstood, that people may not get this drive I had inside of me to create, but that it was right and perfect for me and who I am.

**My inability to be "normal" was simply a vibrant expression of that Creator inside of me.**

# FEED YOUR CREATOR

The ebb. Those times when you have no ideas, you have no desire to create anything. The couch looks perfect...far better than that newsletter you're supposed to write or that book deadline you're about to miss (ahem). I liken it to the doldrums—a ship stranded in the ocean with no breeze to be found, waiting for the breath of God to blow it to shore.

We cannot make the wind blow...
But we can pick up an oar.

## TIME TO PATTERN DISRUPT.

Set things aside and do something counterintuitive.

- Jump in puddles instead of sitting inside watching the rain fall.

- Keep a file of awesome ideas to play with when you are feeling no inspiration.

- Draw instead of creating a client.

- Journal.

- Read.

- Go to a party.

- Play golf.

*Your ability to create is in direct proportion to how **FULL** you feel.*

If you're on empty you won't have anything to create from.
No manna. No life force. No juice.

To be CREATIVE you must fuel your fires.
To create a business you must take time OUT of your business.
To write a book you must take time AWAY from your computer.
To paint a painting you must SEE the world around you.

*You cannot expect to sit down and be brilliant
if you are out of stardust.*

# RE-WRITE THE RULES
# OF GOOD BEHAVIOR

and make the bad decisions that will lead

to the most *fabulous* stories.

# S L O W    D O W N

Yesterday, I read a book that had nothing to do with self growth, inspi-rational blah-blah, goddesses or expansion, and would not be trending amongst my friends.

I cuddled and napped with my granddaughter.
I warmed up dinner instead of cooking it.
I took a shower and didn't shave (tmi?).
I didn't turn on Facebook or check my phone except to read my book on it because it was lighter and less work than my iPad.
I didn't return messages or even acknowledge that I had any.
I didn't write in my book.
I didn't schedule appointments or have deep conversations.
I watched two recorded episodes of *S.H.I.E.L.D.* and at least one of *The Voice*.
I checked out, and it felt great.

I allowed myself to just be irresponsible & unresponsive...cocooning was the most restorative action I could take.

I just had a massive energy output in my business AND I had some really awesome projects emerging. And sometimes I forget to pause. To allow the full expansion to really settle into my bones. To celebrate and NOT do. I rush from one creation to the next without fully appreciating what I've done and who I had to become to be able to do it. Always in a cycle of 'NEXT' instead of appreciating a moment of 'NOW'.

That's where the breakdowns are triggered, when we don't allow the contraction to be easy, when we don't slow down enough to really notice, we suddenly wake up, look around and shock the hell out of our egos who decide to run the stories that don't need to be replayed—those stories that judge us and our situation and keep us stuck and feeling bad.

I remember my first assignment from one of my coaches, July 2013, when we were about to hang up. He called me a tinkerer—always tinkering with something new or reworking something existing. Said it was holding me back from really truly creating something powerful. He assigned me the challenge to do nothing in my business for 2 weeks (other than serve the people who were already on my calendar). To shut down everything for 2 weeks.

## *The inactivity was more painful than childbirth.*

AND it allowed me the space to really analyze where I was and recognize where I was out of alignment, on a path that wasn't the one I wanted to be on. I was so filled with 'next' that I was just nexting my way out of my own message. Those 2 weeks of nothing changed everything for me and opened the doors for my internal world to take the reins. I needed space that I had never allowed myself to actually take.

# PAINT BY NUMBERS

Being an entrepreneur is an art form...never taking the same shape twice, each artist has their own style, their own color preference and medium. As a coach I create my own unique brushstrokes on the souls of my clients. It's an expression of our inner selves and who we are and what we bring to the table. Creating paradigm shifts for others requires us to be fully present and fully, authentically our own powerful selves.

So why are we sitting in a room painting by numbers?
Why are you copying from someone else's canvas?

You want to create art? Well art requires passion and dedication and an overwhelming willingness to break every single rule to make a masterpiece.

You must pick up that brush over and over again to really be able to feel and smell and see the paint in your dreams. To have it embroiled in your essence.

Your business can be beautifully crafted, one color at a time or by splashing all the colors on the canvas and rolling around in it. It's an art form, a great form of expression and emotion.

Create your business as you would a masterpiece.

**Throw away the paint-by-numbers crap.**

Results aren't important to the starter.

**STARTING is.**

# WHAT IF THE NUMBERS OR THE LIKES DIDN'T MATTER?

I've had a coaching blog for years...thoughts and rants...what I felt (in the beginning) I was supposed to blog about. I can trace my own personal progression as a woman and as an entrepreneur reading through them.

Someone asked me yesterday how I have posted at least 2 articles a month for years. "What's your secret to writing so much and getting so many comments and likes?"

If you really want to know how to write more, then I ask—how can you not CARE about writing more? I populate my blog with a living record of my own personal progression as a coach, a person, an author.

It's not a tool for my business, it's a tool for my life. I don't care that I have x many posts or that they are optimized for SEO, and I don't care how many hits I get. (I stopped watching numbers years ago and I've succeeded at higher and higher levels since.) I don't get a bunch of comments or likes on my blog.

I don't write for you. Sorry (not sorry).
I don't write for business.
I write to say the things I just feel like saying.
I write because it helps my Inner Creator feel full.

And yes, sometimes I write about a new program I'm launching or a spot on my coaching roster...because I FEEL like it, not because I feel like I should.

And sometimes I just write what pops into my heart at random moments.

I allow my Creator to have free reign, no restrictions or optimization or goals to convert. Just allowing the words to flow out onto the blank screen.

## RESULTS AREN'T IMPORTANT TO THE STARTER.
Starting is.

**Want to be a better writer?** *Write.*

Write horribly. Write with poor grammar. Write nonsense. Write from your heart.

**Want to be a better blogger?** *Just Be.*

Think of it not as a piece of technology that will get you those magical clients, but as a piece of your soul on display.

**Want to post things on Facebook that everyone loves and comments on?** *Stop trying so hard.*

I've had profound posts that have only had a few likes. And sometimes that stings a little until I realize that the post is about ME not YOU, and then the numbers don't matter.

**Want to create a new program?**
*Create it. Talk to people about what you're creating while you're creating it.*

**I don't write for likes, I write because I CAN.**

The numbers don't matter. The amount of articles don't matter. The number of posts don't matter.

What matters is you, and what creating and writing does for YOU.

## IF THE NUMBERS DIDN'T MATTER, WHAT WOULD YOU SAY?
Say that...

## IF THE RESULTS DIDN'T MATTER, WHAT WOULD YOU START?
Go do that...

# HANDY DANDY
# Cheat Sheet

### REPRESSED + CONSTRICTED CREATOR

- Too many ideas, no action

- Overwhelmed by the first step

- Stuck in inaction

- No trust in your ability to create

- Lose your natural moving state of freedom &
  end up fighting for everything

- Obstinate, unmoving

- Feeling inadequate and incapable

- All force and no flow

FOR THE

# CREATOR & STARTER

## FULLY EXPANDED & EXPRESSED CREATOR

- Lots of ideas and a focus on one at a time

- The first step is made because it's exciting and fun

- Taking inspired action

- Trusting your abilities to create anything

- Stepping powerfully into the nature of life, by experimenting with new ideas and creations that bring more freedom and space for you

- Curious, flexible

- Feeling fear as an indication that moving forward is exactly right

- All flow and no force

# COCREATOR

— AND —

# CONNECTOR

Plays well with others

# *the second seat* 2

Every community, every partnership, every relationship, every client...the CoCreator comes in and finds the optimal, most mutually beneficial way to coexist.

My Inner CoCreator shows up as the one who works well with others, creating amicable agreements and creating things in the world hand in hand with Spirit or with partners. No separation. No strife. No judgment. We create something that works in the highest and best interest of all people.

It's also everything my only child-self isn't, an unselfish team player.

The CoCreator helps my ego to be quiet enough to create direct agreements between my heart, soul and mind, allowing me to be in full alignment with my whole self—like an internal negotiator. So in a way, it's the avenue to cocreating not just with others, but with the Universe as well.

This aspect of me is brilliant at working in harmony with others, lifting them up so we can rise together. I trust my partners because I can see their strengths and play into them, choosing people with the highest vibrations to cocreate solutions with.

Peace for the betterment of all is what this part of me seeks, gaining results without conflict.

*Fully expressed, my CoCreator brings white light to every situation and steps on each blade of grass without bending it.*

Love and light? Yep. But more than that there is also a fierceness to this part of me, a force to be reckoned with—not because life is a fight, but because peaceful coexistence is not always an easy path. Extreme faith and self knowledge and discipline are required to keep the mind and heart pure enough to breathe out the highest and best in each situation. Judgment must be weeded out to fully expand...judgment of situations, judgment of others, judgment of self. The CoCreator is a loving force for balance.

There is a patience to how my CoCreator operates, stepping back from each situation, pulling the mind and emotions away and allowing the divine to flow through every decision. Truly peaceful solutions aren't defined by the absence of strife, but rather by the ability to see the beauty within. And only through slowing down and breathing in Source can the magnificence in each moment be seen.

Here's the thing, my CoCreator is responsible for forming my communities, my friendships, my partnerships, my relationships, and helps my clients succeed time and time again.

Without community, my business would not exist. Without being able to toss aside my judgment, my clients wouldn't feel safe to express who they really are. Without my CoCreator, I wouldn't be able to help them trust themselves more, take their hand and walk the path alongside them.

*The clues that I am repressing the awesomeness of my CoCreator can show up in a few different ways, as a judge or a hermit or even a people pleaser.*

As a judge I am quick to make decisions. I sit upon my pedestal and see nothing but faults in others, or in myself, judging each behavior, each grey hair, each scuff on my shoe. There is no peace within. Life is a constant struggle. I refuse to get the support or see the value in having others along with me for the journey.

**Which also makes me turn into a hermit.**

As an introvert and an only child, being without people is a natural state for me. When it starts feeling unbalanced is when I turn my back on my community, my friends, my family. I sequester myself from the world because I don't want to be with others rather than just enjoying moments of peace and solitude. Usually there's this story that my own company is far superior than those stupid people down the hill (judgy...). Worse, I disconnect from Spirit. I go up into my head and think I can do everything alone.

Peace for the sake of peace is a constricted energy and feels a little like a people-pleaser, the one who solves everything and says yes to every single opportunity for fear of not being liked. As a sacrificial lamb, I give away everything. There is no self-care until others' needs are cared for. I avoid conflict so much that I stomp down my own needs for the sake of peace.

## *I seek to make everyone happy around me and in doing so* I GIVE AWAY MY POWER.

I cannot make a decision that doesn't take other people's needs into account regardless of what my own needs are. I give and give and give until my own resources have run dry, and then I fill them up for the sole purpose of giving more away. While I am creating a peaceful existence for others I miss the greatest piece of my purpose, which is to bring peace into the world through me, not at my own expense, not by suppressing my magnificence, but by serving the world from a place of fullness.

*Hand in hand with the Universe*
*or with others is the path to success.*

What a fully expanded Connector brings to my life is a richness that couldn't be felt alone.

I'm a brilliant capable person, and my CoCreator reminds me that my awesomest is 10-fold more powerful if I understand that I don't need to travel this path alone.

# TAKE MY HAND

Take my hand,
walk beside me.
Create a better world,
Not from behind me or by following my footsteps, but by carrying a scythe
to cut the path with me.

For as a I clear the path, so can you walk on it.
And as you clear the path, so can I walk on it.
We can take turns.

There is no need to lead.
There is no need to follow.
There is no need to compare blades or paths.
There is no need to deem one of us a winner.
There is no need to categorize how we walk, talk, dress, wear our hair, act,
speak or whatever.

We will celebrate each other's successes as if they were our own.
We will pick each other up and dust each other off.
We will wait patiently while the other grieves.
We will leap off of a cliff trusting the other to be there to catch us.
We will laugh with our whole body, tears of joy combining with the pain in
our stomachs as it is infused with the lightness of our togetherness.
We will encourage, support, believe in, and SEE each other.

Together we can create peace on the planet...

The foundation of ANY successful business isn't found in the product or marketing, but in the ability to create a community of people who KNOW, TRUST AND **LOVE** YOU.

End world hunger...

Place a roof over every human's head...

Create a hippy-dippy-prada-wearing culture of abundance and social responsibility.

Or simply sit and BE

Hand in hand

Hearts filled with love and gratitude,

Fully aware of

Just how lucky

We are

To have found each other

Again

In

This

Lifetime...

# THE POWER OF COMMUNITY

I was getting married to my husband and my in-laws-to-be gave me a call. Their friends wanted to throw me a wedding shower.

Sitting in that room filled with strangers I was struck by how much love was present. These women raised their children together and had been connected for over 35 years. They were a community of support gathered together to truly celebrate the joy of one of their own.

And I wondered what that would be like. I wondered what it would be like to have neighbors that I didn't California-wave to as I rushed into my garage without having to have a conversation. Community that I could count on in an emergency. Community I could count on to share laughter and tears and frustrations. Not just friends—circles of friends.

*These women wrote
the stories of their lives together.*

And a little piece of my wall broke down that day never to be replaced. I was shown just how valuable, no, just how ESSENTIAL it is in life to have a circle of people who are just...there, connected.

# Community is the foundation of life.

It's the foundation of ANY business.

It's the secret to raising children, having friendships, getting support and making money.

What if we were to litter the pages of other people's stories by simply being **open to the connection** that community brings?

# PASSIVE COMMUNICATION

I'm not interested in passive interaction.

Give me passion and connection. Give me conversation and interest.

And I'll bring that to the table, too.

Don't see me as another number who 'likes' you or your post or your page.

Don't add me to groups without asking my permission.

Don't send me emails and hope I see them.

Don't hand me your card and wait for me to call.

**CONNECT** with me!

And I'll do the same for you.

We get lazy.

We start sending out mass messages in the hope that one person will take it personally.

I get lazy.

I do the same thing sometimes.

Like sending an email newsletter and assuming my work for the day is done.

But it's not.

As a CoCreator, I know that there's one more thing I have to do, the thing that is a non-negotiable in my workday...and that's to connect personally with ONE person.

Not hundreds or thousands.
One.
That's the opposite of passive.

I'm an introvert.
Even introverts need connection.
Heart to heart, soul to soul connection.

The more separated from humanity I am, the more my CoCreator withers in the corner, sad and alone.

I can shout from an empty room all day long and still that would be passive.
Connection takes EFFORT.

People are rarely truly SEEN.
Be the one to SEE them.
Eye to eye, knee to knee seeing.

We can support ourselves.
We can counsel ourselves.
We can do it ourselves.

We don't have to though...

# TRUST AND CONTROL

*"You have issues with control. You wake up and try to control how your life is Co-Created with the Universe. You say, 'Universe please help me create this life' and then you say, 'but only deliver it between the hours of 8–10 and knock 3 times when you get here'. And every time you think you know better than the Universe, you effectively push it away."*

Some conversations with my Spiritual Coach are more painful than others.

The hardest sessions are always the ones when she speaks the truth that cuts me to my core.

This was one of those.

It also wasn't the first time **CONTROL** came up...

**My need to control how Spirit shows up, what it needs to look like and when I choose to allow it to come forward was the very thing that was holding me back in my life the most.** Control makes me feel safe. It soothes my rational mind. If I release control then I am automatically the opposite—out of control, spinning in the world with no personal responsibility or accountability.

And without TRUST, I cannot expand.

Do I trust myself to let go of controlling my surroundings, circumstances, appearance, what I do and say and pretend to be?

Do I trust my inner voice enough to listen to it all of the time, not just when it is convenient?

Do I trust Source enough to let it flow through me, not as a pet to be leashed and walked, but as a part of me?

Do I trust my loved ones to still love me if I do?

The more I control, the less I trust.
The more I trust, the less I need to control.

*And in order to cocreate my life
hand in hand with the Universe,
I must release the control, and trust.*

In any relationship, trust is the foundation.
In any relationship, control destroys.

Why would my relationship to Spirit be any different?
Why would my relationship to myself be any different?

# GETTING SUPPORT TO HELP YOU COCREATE

*I could do it myself because only I know the right way.*
**I welcome support because there might be ways I haven't seen.**

*I could do it myself because it'll be faster if I don't have to explain it.*
**I welcome support because quality is more important than speed.**

*I could do it myself because the vision is only in MY head.*
**I welcome support because I love being a visionary, but the details bore me.**

*I could do it myself because I can't afford support.*
**I welcome support because I can grow my income exponentially without having to get bogged down with tasks.**

*I could do it myself because I don't want to manage anyone.*
**I welcome support because the right person partners with me, shares my vision, and holds me to it.**

*I could do it myself because I've never done it any other way.*
**I welcome support because trying new ways is exciting and fun.**

*I could do it myself because I don't want to bother anyone.*
**I welcome support because people WANT to support me if only I'd ask.**

Without trust, I cannot

E X P A N D

# DON'T HIDE

Don't hide behind the technology and then wonder what's going on.

Facebook, Twitter, websites...they are all simply technology.

They are not a strategy, they are tools for expression.

YOU are the strategy. YOU are the expression.
Do you want to powerfully create clients?
Are you willing to show up powerfully?

## CONNECT.

# HANDY DANDY
# *Cheat Sheet*

## REPRESSED & CONSTRICTED COCREATOR

- Judgmental, seeing nothing but faults in others or in yourself

- Unable to work with others

- Refuse to get support or see the value of having others along for the journey

- Turn your back on community, friends, family, sequester yourself

- People-pleasing, solving everything and saying yes to everything for fear of not being liked

- Give away everything

- No self-care until others' needs are taken care of

- Avoids conflict of all kinds

# FOR THE
# COCREATOR & CONNECTOR

## FULLY EXPANDED & EXPRESSED COCREATOR

- Accepting, seeing the beauty and divinity in others and in yourself

- Loves working alongside others (and with Source)

- Values the energy of others and builds a team to support any and all efforts

- Appreciates alone time and time with others equally

- Understands that all people have their own journey and serves willingly without servitude

- Gives lovingly and on purpose

- Self-care is the highest form of service to be able to give to others

- Understanding that not everyone agrees with everyone all of the time, but disagreement is not an indicator of ill will

# CATALYST

— AND —

# ENROLLER

C'mon Baby Light My Fire

# the third seat

Enthusiasm comes from the Greek root *entheos* and means *filled with God*. The enthusiasm of the Catalyst is what drives this force within you.

You know how you're sitting there watching TV and an infomercial comes on? One minute you have no need for a widget that super charges your cooking time and the next you've just spent 45 minutes watching the show and you're on hold on the phone to order yourself not one, but two widgets with the special bonuses.

You were just *enrolled* by their *enthusiasm*.

The Inner Catalyst is the spark. It's the place where every enrolling conversation begins.

Need your husband to be on board with buying a new couch? Out comes the Catalyst to appeal to the part of him that just wants to make you happy.

Need to enroll clients? Enroll employees? The Catalyst is the negotiator that makes those beginnings and adventures possible.

We are on a mission from God—Blues Brothers style.

*This aspect is not about cheerleading or empty smiles or placating words.*

**THE CATALYST IS COMMITTED TO PASSION—**
finding passion and lighting it up so that we are fully INTO the cause. Because the more fully invested we are in the cause, the more readily we can throw others into battle mode, gripped with a fever so powerful and meaningful that they can no longer hold back.

**THE CATALYST INSPIRES ACTION.**
In fact, the Catalyst makes such an impassioned case that NOT acting becomes impossible.

*The Catalyst holds the lighter that inspires us to grow and expand into greater levels of consciousness...*

Or greater levels of success...
Or greater levels of focus...
Or greater levels of freedom...
Or whatever greater level of
being-ness we are desiring.

## IT'S THE JUMPSTARTER OF ACTION THAT IS UNDENIABLE...

When we're fully aligned with the Inner Catalyst we are expressive, joyous, fired up, inspired, passionate. We're able to see and feel the bigger picture and are the fullest, biggest version of US.

When we really lean in, fully in alignment with our hearts' desires, we enroll others by being enthused about the path we're walking. We are able to really channel our emotion into a specific direction with focus, clarity and strength of purpose.

*But when we're not in alignment,*
*when we suppress the Catalyst's energy,*
*we feel scattered.*

We are filled with worry or depression. We become prone to fits of crying or anger, to emotions stuck without a proper channel. Our message is LOST, missing.

We ramble and skirt issues. And we are frustrated. We are frustrated that others aren't engaged with what we're saying, and we are frustrated that we know we're not saying what's really inside of us.

And we complain and wallow in negative emotion or worse, we become a shallow emotionless hull of ourselves and come from a place of emptiness without passion.

**Without our Inner Catalyst, we are stuck without words when all we really want to do is explain.**

So how do we let the Catalyst out?
How do we let the passion come through?

It's simple.

# WE NEED TO **BE CLEAR** ABOUT WHAT WE WANT.

That's when the Catalyst shines! That's when you attract the very things you most want to attract, when you can build your business and your life with joy and enthusiasm.

When the feelings and emotions we most need to express come out of us and go into the world—that's the magic.

# LET'S BE MEDIOCRE

*My greatest dream in life is to be completely and totally mediocre...*
Says no one...ever.

We may not all reach for stardom or fame. We may be happy playing on the sidelines, being in charge of the lights and sound. We may want to live a perfectly normal Norman Rockwell kind of life.

*But in our heart of hearts,*
**we don't wish for mediocre.**

And yet who among us is truly reaching outside of that middle lane?
Are we willing to speak our truth with power and conviction?
Are we willing to show the world our passion? Our power? Our vulnerabilities? Our successes? Our failures?

**Are we willing to unabashedly, shamelessly be ourselves?**

Is there a tiny little pyromaniac inside of each of us ready to light fire to the pages of our story just so that we can dance in the shifting light of the blazing flame for one night of wild abandon?

**Light the damn match and ignite your soul.**
Light them all.

**Tear down the damn walls holding you in, holding you back.**
Tear them down.

Say all the wrong things.
Act inappropriately.
Dance naked (metaphorically or physically).
Write without editing and use your and you're incorrectly.
Laugh at the wrong places.
Grab your lover's hand and don't let go.
Scream for everyone to hear.
Talk about your success with pride, and talk about your failures with equal pride.
Love your shadow as much as your light.

In one blink of the eye, your flame can be extinguished, a mere blip in the infinity of time.

*Will your legacy be that you always played it safe and died mediocre?*

*Or will your legacy be that you* **LIVED**, *full-out, dancing in the light?*

# FOLLOW THE JOY?

Today I raise the battle flags: **do nothing that isn't from your heart's desire in your business.**

Nay-sayers say that won't work.

They say you have to do stuff you don't like.

They say you must follow a clearly defined plan and walk the path tread upon by others.

They say that to be a successful entrepreneur you need to conform.

They say that at the same time they are raising their own flags screaming that they have a magical formula to help you be more authentic, spiritual, rich.

## I SAY THEY ARE WRONG.

I say that sounds a lot like being employed by others.

I say that your SEO, numbers of followers, your capacity to follow other people's instructions means jack-diddly if your heart isn't fully 1,000% engaged.

I say outsource the stuff you don't like and chase the passion...

Silence your brain and toss out all the lessons you've learned about blindly following what works for others.

# BE THE CATALYST IN YOUR BUSINESS.

Let your passion and enthusiasm seep into every decision, every action, every piece of your business.

*What would happen if* you stopped worrying about saying the right thing and just spoke?

*What would happen if* you stopped having sales conversations and simply had conversations?

*What would happen if* you stopped trying to market and learned to create clients intuitively and through your true spiritual, heart center?

*What would happen if* you created more space for yourself to create instead of creating more tasks to do?

*What if* you set out to create more deep connections rather than make more prospects?

*What would happen if* you did what came easy and still stretched into your edge?

*What would happen if* your entire business plan could be summed up in one sentence...the mission that wakes you up in the morning?

*What would it look like* to be the person who truly followed the songs of joy and whispers of passion in the recesses of your heart?

# DO WE REALLY NEED TO KNOW WHY?

Do I need to know why I love the color blue for it to soothe my soul?

Do I need to know why I love the Meyer lemons from my tree to fully enjoy them?

Do I need to know why when my dog looks at me with those love eyes and I can't help but scratch his neck to show just how much I love him?

And yet entrepreneurs are constantly pushed to find out why they are creating their business.

**Does it really matter?**

What if we just KNOW.

What if we know we have a vision and it just feels right and we WANT it.

We can feel the passion.

We can feel the excitement.

**Do we need to know why?**

I paint my walls blue.

I eat those sweet and sour lemons.

I pet and kiss and love on my dog.

I create that project.

Can it be that simple? Do we really need more than that?

When someone comes up to me and asks me what my **BIG WHY** is, my answer is simply

## *"because it feels really flipping good, because I WANT to, because my Inner Enthusiast LOVES to."*

Why? **Because I CAN.**

And really, the sexier question for me then becomes, "WHY NOT?"

Beyond the hype...
Beyond what you're being **told** to do...

What is it that...
Rocks
You
To
Your
Core?

# KICKING THE CHEERLEADER

When a scientist gets up and is excited for a project it's noble.

When a cheerleader gets up and is super-duper excited for her team even when they are losing, I guarantee that someone in the crowd secretly wants to kick her in the teeth.

## ENTHUSIASM TRIGGERS PEOPLE.

Being enthusiastic pokes at the upper limits of how much happiness is socially acceptable.

## HOW MUCH HAPPINESS IS SOCIALLY ACCEPTABLE?

It's okay for someone with special needs to laugh loudly in the middle of the library for no reason.

It's not okay for a scholar to do the same thing when she reads a funny finding in the tomes on her desk.

It's okay for a child to ask questions, be curious, approach life with the enthusiasm of a beginner's mind, to stop and look at a drop of dew on a grass blade and giggle when she falls.

It's not acceptable for an adult to look at everything in the world as new. He is expected to know things and he must demonstrate that knowingness to be accepted and successful.

## HOW PASSIONATE CAN WE BE WITHOUT BEING DEEMED MANIACAL?

How demonstrative can we be around the wonders of the universe without being asked to take a drug test?

When is our own tolerance of enthusiasm stretched past what we deem acceptable?

What do we need to do to raise the bar on how much enthusiasm we can exude?

*Repressing your energy in one area means all areas are missing out on the energy behind the damn dam.*

**SET IT FREE.**

# SHOWING UP YOU

You know what makes you attractive to clients?
It's not using the right buzz-words.
It's not how many followers you have.
It's not having great photos.
It's not creating the most beautimus website and logo.
It's not crafting a tag-line or marketing materials that stick.

## IT'S SHOWING UP.

Showing up powerfully as you.
Showing up vulnerably as you.
Showing up in integrity as you.
Showing up aligned as you.
Showing up and making mistakes.
Showing up and being unprofessional.

It's taking all the compartmentalized pieces of you, the ones you've stashed away in neat little boxes, labeled 'business me', 'spiritual me', 'parent me', 'wife/husband me', 'football crazy screaming fan me' and dumping all those boxes out onto the floor, smushing them all together, and presenting the messy wholeness of YOU.

You know what enrolls clients time and time and time again?
You being YOU.
You holding nothing back.

# The most catalytic parts of you

## DON'T COME WITH A LABEL.

Those are the pieces that make you irresistible for others who are busy wasting their energy filling their boxes, waiting for someone to show them how to return to wholeness.

# JUST QUIT

I have a friend who used to be in the mortgage business. Like clockwork every 4–6 months one of us would call the other to quit. We would quit and then we would talk about what else we were going to do. What new adventure we'd go on. And we'd resign officially to each other. And a few days later we'd feel better and come back to work.

It wasn't about quitting as much as it was about **releasing the pressure of continuing.** It would break our momentum and allow us to reboot.

I still do that. I allow myself to reboot.

You see, the less I do, the less in my brain I am. Boredom ensues. And boredom is death, especially for creative minds. It's like experiencing a real-life version of writers block, and it sucks...

*When the fires of my Catalyst are set to low, I drift.*

I could keep pushing.

I could stay there forcing myself to feel passionate, sticking with it even without being excited about it.

But that wouldn't be me.

I feel that sometimes we need to create space and perspective. We need to stop pushing. We NEED to walk away. Our souls are pressed up against our brains so hard that neither can breathe.

So quit.

Go for it.

Hand me your resignation letter, and I promise to process it for you.

You can rehire yourself later, when you've allowed your sabbatical to run it's course. You will know when it's time...you can wait until you start to feel your smile unfurling the sails in your heart.

Slow down.

Don't fight it.

Go chop some fresh wood so when you're ready, you can reignite your Inner Catalyst and kick some fresh ass.

# HANDY DANDY
## Cheat Sheet

### REPRESSED & CONSTRICTED CATALYST

- Scattered emotionally and mentally

- Filled with worry or depression

- Feeling lost

- Skirts issues

- Frustrated because there is no way to express powerfully what's really inside of you

- Complaining constantly

- Shallow, emotionless hull of emptiness without passion

- Lacking direction to do anything meaningful in life

# FOR THE
# CATALYST & ENROLLER

## FULLY EXPANDED & EXPRESSED CATALYST

- Expressive, joyous, fired up, inspired, passionate

- Able to see and feel the bigger picture

- Being the fullest biggest version of yourself

- Enrolling others because of how easily you share the passion of your journey

- Able to channel emotion into a specific direction with focus, clarity, and strength of purpose

- Becomes a person on a mission

- Super clear in talking about what you truly desire

# LEADER

— AND —

# MANAGER

Take me to your leader, and
who's really in charge here?

# the fourth seat

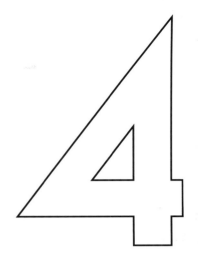

Great leaders LEAD others towards a vision, they inspire and allow for course corrections, they take input from others and allow the project to evolve and grow. They see the biggest possibilities and they break them down into next steps.

Great leaders don't control their resources, they enhance and lift them up. They call out to the greatness within others and hold them to that higher vision...that's what my Inner Leader does.

This aspect marches for freedom and abundance and service and fights for the whole—for the wholeness of who you are.

The Leader finishes things for me, project-manages and allocates my inner resources.

Life is a process, always changing, always moving, and my Leader keeps things flowing both in a big-picture way and in a detail-oriented way as well: Here is the big picture, and here is the inspired action we'll be taking today; here is where our passion lies, and here is the path we'll be taking.

If each day we were only to meet with one of our inner guides, this would be the one who would help us see what propels us to greater heights.

Today, to whom do we need to be more loving? What do we need to feel more joy? And if we took any action today to bring us more freedom, what would it look like?

*Communicating with the Inner Leader*
*is like having a daily staff meeting.*

Breathe deeply and **CONNECT.**

# *What does the Leader need today so that we can create what we most want to create?*

We need someone running the ship or everything seems to fall apart. The Leader is the glue that holds it all together, allowing all aspects of us to work together seamlessly. Whether we're managing a household schedule or leading a client into deeper insights on a coaching call, this is the aspect that oversees our life. The Leader allows us to see the resources all around and within us so we can keep moving smoothly through life.

All things can be possible, and the Leader knows this. The Leader uses all parts of the puzzle to create a brighter picture. It's not about striving for order or perfection.

Through the eyes of the leader, we never ever assume anything is broken, but that every event or situation is simply an opportunity for growth. We don't judge good or bad, perfection or imperfection, but recognize that it is all part of the cosmic plan. Through this plan, we can lean into the chaos and still feel internally peaceful. In this peace, we can trust that we know what step to take next.

# The biggest stuff only gets done when our Inner Leader has been released.

This is the stuff that propels us to our greatest purpose, a purpose we are fully invested in.

We have a mission statement, and the Leader makes sure that our entire being is in alignment with that statement above all else. Challenges come up, but the Leader doesn't worry about them, and instead helps us find solutions, allowing the challenges to become inconsequential in the greater scheme of things. We learn from the challenges, rise above them, and keep moving forward no matter what.

**In constricted form** we can be a little OCD and a perfectionist, judging all things that don't follow the standard methodology. When we try to control things and we know there is only one right way then we also know our Inner Leader is out of alignment, that we're trying to force instead of allowing things to unfold.

And what if your Inner Manager is out of alignment in a different way? What if it just needs some love? That shows up differently...when we feel disorganized, and feel behind, frazzled or completely overwhelmed. In my life, this shows up as losing track of my keys or forgetting to call the doctor or simply not paying attention to the little details of my life.

When we see and experience these signs they are evidence that we need to give more love to our Manager and allow ourselves to really do the things that nurture us. For me, this might look like putting my cell phone somewhere intentionally and remembering clearly where it is without having to call it.

Whether it's the forcing of things or the lack of centeredness—it just means that we need to pause and allow the Leader to take over...to take our hand.

*With our Inner Leader at the helm, we can trust that surrender is a powerful place.*

# BE AT 100%

Do you just feel tired? Like showing up 100% all of the time would be exhausting? Perhaps 75% feels more realistic. Perhaps showing up sometimes at 100% and other times at 30% feels better, to show up in waves.

Perhaps 100% means being all pretty and shiny all the time, perhaps having your laser vision turned on high all day, getting more done than humanly possible, going, going, going....

Here's the thing—what if showing up 100% wasn't about an intensity or a super-human ability? What if showing up 100% meant to BE YOU and what you're present to fully in every moment? If you're sad, allowing yourself to BE SAD, to let the tears wash over and through you instead of pretending you're happy-happy-joy-joy? If you're happy or proud or serving or reading...can you be 100% into it?

No judgement or stories.
No holding back because of whatever.
No secret business strategies running in the background.
No searching for the magic easy button.
No striving to be something other than you.
No chatter in the backdrop.

Just you and your own 100%.
Full presence in whatever you're experiencing.

*Here's the magic in that...*
## it actually takes more energy to show up with less than 100%.

When we show up at anything less it means we're splitting ourselves into parts.

We spend extra energy holding back.

We spend extra energy multitasking.

We don't use our resources to their fullest & it hurts us.

When we show up with less, it makes our Inner Manager cranky and resentful. We run around wrapping up our resources in incomplete projects or mindless dribble that gets us nowhere, and our resources cannot be reallocated until we release those incompletions or we complete them.

**We can't complete anything if our resources are split.**

But if we complete things, our energy is released back into us. It frees us to move forward with our dreams.

# WHAT'S YOUR REAL LEGACY

Taking on MORE doesn't earn you more. Having a long to-do list is an illusion you've created to make it seem like you know what the heck you're doing each day.

*Your long to-do lists do **nothing** for your bottom line—they just make you busy.*

If you want to be busy go for it.

But...

What if instead of doing the busy work and having the long to-do list, you decided to do something different. **What if you decided to do the things that are the most valuable to you and your business?**

# BEST GIFT EVER

*"Isn't it hard to work?"*

I have lost track of how many people have asked that of me since my Granddaughter was born.

*"Doesn't having your Granddaughter in the house while working from home make it harder to get stuff done?"*

I'm happy to say, yes...AND no.

Yes, I want to cuddle up with her and play.
Yes, I want to be available to help my daughter all of the time.
Yes, it's a distraction when I'm trying to do deep work to hear that little voice start to cry.

AND having her around has been amazing for my business BECAUSE she is a distraction. I no longer have the luxury of doing things that are extra, that are optional, that are me just filling the work day.

See if I really want to go cuddle or help my daughter or read some Dr. Seuss to Lizzie, then I gotta get stuff done. I have to be committed to focusing on the most important task only. There's not time for fluff or surfing. There's no space for losing track of time. I gotta get in and create magic time and time again—no room for anything less.

*My Inner Leader needs to step up and*
*LEAD my day in the most powerful way possible.*

And I'll tell you what—**the less I do, the more success-ful I become.** I have never proposed more or created more in a condensed period of time, and it's all because my desire to play is so prevalent. I can hear her little voice in the background calling to me. I can feel myself sliding into a flow state, where work just becomes easy.

I'll tell you one more thing that was unexpected for me—I **no longer see my success as something op-tional,** as something that I want, but have never full-heartedly committed to. I feel as if I never really felt that urge to create a legacy with my business. Not that I'm not passionate about coaching and writing, I completely am and love my work, it's just that being a mother and building my lifestyle was my top priority, and my work was always something that was optional.

But suddenly I'm staring into the face of my grand-daughter, realizing that my only responsibility to her is showering her with pure unadulterated love and lead-ing by example, showing her what is possible on the planet. I don't have to worry about feeding schedules or teacher meetings, I don't have to be inundated with the details of parenting. I just get to BE the person who simply loves.

It was like looking in the face of my own mortality in a way, wondering what I would be able to show her, knowing that she'd be studying me with different eyes as well. I'm the person she'll go to as a teen when she's sparring with her mother. I'm the person she'll go to when she wants to eat the forbidden foods. I'm the person who will sit and read her book after book after book without getting up to clean the house.

I'm also the person that she may someday have to bury.

What will I have shown her?

*I hope to show her that life is filled with infinite possibilities, and I believe in each of them for her* **AS I HAVE DONE FOR MYSELF.**

So if you ask what this little being has done to rock my world, it's simple. There's no waiting until the kids are grown and gone to really push the limits of my business. The time is NOW.

And there is no limit to how much love I can give. There's no holding back...Heart wide-open, staring into those big questioning eyes, knowing that these are the moments Grandmas are made for.

So to answer the questions around how hard it is to have a baby in the house while I'm working...

**BEST GIFT EVER.**

If you want to be a great leader, start internally.

Support, Lift Up, and Guide Yourself without judgment or strife.

# BAD LEADERS DON'T EXIST

Someone asked me once what a bad leader looked like,
and I paused and replied,

*"There are no bad leaders.*
*There are ineffectual people in positions of power,*
*but they aren't leaders."*

And I place that here in this aspect of myself to remember. I need to remember that when I'm truly coming from a place of leadership—in my life, in my business, and in my interactions with others—magic happens.

When I don't, I simply become ineffectual. I cannot properly use the resources around me or within me if I'm not leading in my life. I have to be willing to lift others up and speak to THEIR Inner Leader and promote that higher level of self-responsibility in us all.

It is through deeper levels of leadership that my work as a coach, as a parent, as a wife, as a whatever label I'm wearing, takes on an ease and flow. No conflict— just a deep trust that the next step will be the right divine one.

# SACRED ROUTINES

We did a garage conversion project in our home. The contractors took off the whole wall where the garage door used to be and framed out the new wall in one day. These guys came in and just blew through the work. Suddenly garage lights were replaced with new can lights, a spot for the ceiling fan, the ventilation system was installed, and the door was lifted to match the new floor.

In one day, a garage looked like an apartment.

We were talking, and these guys are thinking that they could be done in a week if it weren't for the inspections. A week for what we thought would be at least a month.

Why? Because they do this all the time. They know each other so well that they even do most of it without having to talk to each other. They just go in, everyone knows what to do, and they do it.

*They don't over complicate it or create new ways of doing anything.*

## THEY SHOW UP,
## DO WHAT THEY'VE GOTTA DO,
## AND THEY MOVE ON.

And they love it. They love seeing the projects evolve. The process is creative to them because each project, while the steps might be the same, is totally different.

Wonder what would happen if you got so good at creating clients that you'd just show up, get shit done, and move on?

Wonder what would happen if you had so much expertise that you knew exactly what to do without second guessing?

Wonder what would happen if we knew the experience would be different each time, but the steps were just second nature?

Yeah, I'm talking about consistency...one of my most dreaded words. Visions of boringness dance through my head.

I have pretty-shiny syndrome with the best of them.

*I don't always like to stick it out*
*to the point of mastery.*

When I do?

I'll admit it, when I practice some form of consistency, my business explodes and the amount of free time I have increases.

But I don't call it consistency, because honestly, consistency makes my skin crawl just a little.

It's a fine line for me. Because there are two types of consistency. There's the kind that feels like taking a ramming rod and hitting it against a 10-foot-wide concrete and steel wall. Forced and Painful Consistency.

That's not sexy. It doesn't call to me. In fact it makes me want to run and hide.

And there's a second way...Creating sacred routines.

I don't manage control
of myself or others.

I manage my soul
over my ego.

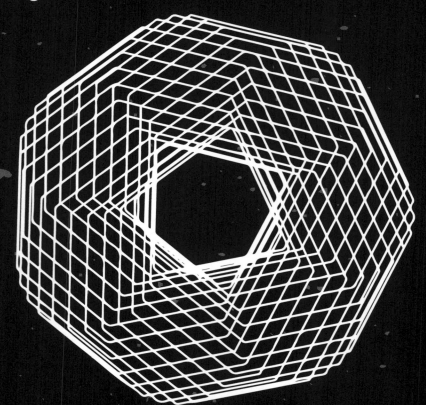

## How can my Inner Leader support the big picture mission? The big dreams?

What if instead of forcing and controlling the process, we create a space where the process becomes natural and feels good?

Sometimes it's easy to say that I'm not feeling inspired to write or to work, easy to push it off for other more 'important' tasks. But I forget that sometimes I don't HAVE the words until I sit down and open up to them.

I wonder what would happen if I simply created a sacred routine to just sit down and write?

Not when the mood struck me, but because it's a part of my day that feels really good; sitting in bed in the early morning with my hot coffee at my bedside, allowing space for the words to come through. And some days the words don't come. And others they flow. Either way, I am willing to create the sacred routine morning after morning so the expression is always able to come through.

I wonder what would happen in my business if I created a sacred routine to reach out to others? I wonder what would happen in my marriage if I created a sacred routine to spend time each day just sending my husband loving thoughts? I wonder what would happen in my spiritual life if I created a sacred routine of putting one of my beautiful hand-made malas in my fingers to feel each of the 108 stones as I chanted the chants my Grandmother taught me when I was a little girl?

Creating sacred routines sets me up powerfully to stay in FLOW, in alignment with my intuition AND create a structure for the redundant to become something special.

# REFORMING MARTHA STEWART

We bought old camera canisters with the film still waiting inside to be used, and then we carefully pulled out some of the film. Painstakingly, I cut the printed birthday party information to the exact size of the exposed film and glued it on, laying it flat overnight so it wouldn't crinkle. In the morning, I rolled them back up, inserted the rolls into the canisters, put them into a decorated bag and popped it into my daughter's backpack.

How *else* would you invite kids to a movie night birthday party?

Had Pinterest been around at the time, **those invitations totally would have gone viral.**

It wasn't my first foray into Martha Stewart-esque behavior. No one else in the family could decorate the big tree at Christmas because it had to be done just so, with the colors being evenly distributed around the whole tree. And then there was that dark year where I decided to hand paint all of the ornaments with a glitter and glue mixture to make it sparkle more. (Working with glitter is for the dedicated and insane).

I'd love to sit here and tell you that there was an emptiness in my soul that only perfection would fill...but that wasn't really it.

**I just thought that was the way I was supposed to be.**

I mean having almost memorized Mary Poppins and being a long-time subscriber to *Martha Stewart Magazine* (and eventually her other publications), oh and being a Virgo, it seemed only natural.

## I needed to be "practically perfect in every way."

Until I finally realized that I really didn't give a shit about ever making that *Bon Appetit* from scratch triple chocolate toffee 5 layer cake—with chocolate whipped cream frosting that makes it nearly impossible to balance the layers—ever again. I'd already made it at least a dozen times. Once would have been enough.

It went downhill from there.
I started to question if anyone really cared.
I served them a cake from a box with frosting from a can.
My traitorous family told me it was the best cake I'd ever made.

I started to question what else I was over-managing.

Did my son remember his farm themed 2nd birthday complete with crafts and games on the grass and a perfectly timed schedule for each of the 6 different stations?

He didn't.
No one really cared that I went to extremes to appear to be perfect.
So why did I?

If everything I did up to this point was in perfect control, what would happen if it weren't? What would happen if I were able to allow?

I started experimenting with that. I spent more time relaxing with my friends and family. I started letting go of the pages and pages of to-do lists. In fact, I stopped making them altogether (eventually...that was a tough one to let go of).

Letting go of the need to be perfect left a lot more space for me to be human, and actually, **I started trusting myself more.** I started trusting that I would do the essential things and everything else was icing on the cake.

The kids survived.

My husband survived (and to this day objects to any from-scratch baked goods from me other than my fresh berry crumbles).

I didn't lose friends over it.

I didn't lose my sense of purpose in life (because really, being perfect isn't a life purpose).

And most importantly,

*I survived.*

# HANDY DANDY
## Cheat Sheet

### REPRESSED & CONSTRICTED LEADER

- A little OCD, control-freakish

- Life micromanager with checklists and checklists for the checklists

- Completely disorganised, frazzled and overwhelmed

- Ineffectual and ignored

- Inflexible because there is a right way and all other ways are wrong

- Only has mistrust in other people's abilities

- Overbearing

- Or a doormat

# FOR THE
# LEADER & MANAGER

## FULLY EXPANDED & EXPRESSED LEADER

- Knows what to do next without over analyzing it

- Keeps in alignment with the big picture

- Utilizes the best resources for each part of the process

- Motivates others to also step-up and lead

- Always open to more powerful ways of doing things

- Inclusive, sees the potential in others

- Stands firm for the greater good

- Gets things done easily and with the appropriate help

# CHANGE
# AGENT

— AND —

# MAVERICK

Put your stake in the ground
and shake up the status quo

# *the fifth seat*

It isn't enough for the Change Agent to simply make change. We need to BE the change. If the highest outcome is to help others lead their lives from a more spiritual source, then sure as hell, we need to step into that more ourselves.

If we take a stand against domestic violence then we need to step up and help others who are creating that shift in consciousness. It's not enough to WANT the change. The Change Agent needs to step in and step up to be that change day in and day out.

It's not always world-change either. The Change Agent wishes to also bring about new ways of doing everything for the betterment of all. Perhaps it's a more efficient way to clean our kitchens, or a faster route to the store—whatever breaks us out of comfortable routines is usually spurred on by this aspect of ourselves. Never stagnating, never settling, and never accepting that there is just one way of doing things.

Change isn't always wanted, it isn't always fun, it isn't always the 'right' timing or what we thought would happen, but changes from our expanded Change Agent are always, always for our highest good and demand an elevated amount of trust and faith. We work in unison with the Universe to give us exactly what we ask for, to help us be of service in the world, and to help us grow as people.

# Without change there can be no growth.

When we constrict the Change Agent, we are resistant to change, fearful of anything outside of our comfort zones. We know there's more to life, but we just can't seem to break out of our existing mindset to do anything about it. We'll just stick with the status quo rather than rock the boat or row anywhere else.

Or on the flip-side, we're unable to commit to anything but change, even when the change is harmful or not necessary. We will change just for the sake of change, appearing to others to be flaky or noncommittal. We'll quit a job after 2 hours because someone calls us to go to a concert with them.

We will not allow ourselves to be grounded or solid, and instead will be constantly seeking out anything or anywhere other than where we are at this moment.

When we allow full expansion of the Change Agent, we ARE grounded and powerful. As a Maverick, we seek out the change that betters us, not the change that is an escape. We become very intentional and powerful in the type of change we seek out, and it comes from a pure heart of service for the betterment of ourselves and others.

# TEENAGE REBELLION & RIGHTEOUS INDIGNATION

In high school I was filled with righteous indignation. Captain of my school's Mock Trial Team, a passionate student of the world's most downtrodden, I went into college as an International Relations major with a minor in Legal Studies. I was all set to go out into the world as an International Lawyer, fighting for the rights of people who were unable to fight for themselves. I was always leading with my Change Agent.

*See a wrong;*
*work to make it right.*

I understood the power of protest. I witnessed riots in Los Angeles and other cities and volunteered to help clean up the broken glass and debris afterwards, starting to comprehend something very important—the Change Agent didn't always have to be fighting to create change in the world.

I will admit that there were years when my Change Agent was depressed and disillusioned. That the task I set out to achieve didn't look nearly as glamorous as I had thought. I had failed to truly effect change because I had failed to see the larger picture of the world, where black and white don't necessarily exist. It seemed too big for one person to change the entire world, even as my application for the Peace Corps was in the process of being completed.

Suddenly there came a point when I didn't know exactly what I was fighting for, and I shut down my Change Agent for many years, settling instead for a life filled with compliance and complacency.

As I matured and learned new ways to influence and model change, my Inner Change Agent went through transformations as well.

I realized if I only change one life, I can create a tidal wave of change. That is the highest service I can provide the world.

My relationship with my Change Agent has taken many different turns. It's the source of all my maverick tendencies, which meant teenage rebellion and walking out of jobs because my boss dared to question me. It's totally the part of me that still to this day doesn't like to be told what to do.

It's also a huge part of ME, of my power, and of my mission. My "people" are fighting for the same thing, for freedom from the formulas that dictate how we lead our lives and our businesses.

When I speak through this aspect of myself I say things like:

I want to change the face of coaching...
I want to create a new breed of coaches...
I help people learn to trust their own inner voice so that they can throw off the shackles of the 'shoulds' and live into who they are meant to be...

Or even my business motto: **SCREW THE FORMULAS.**

It's the part of me that still desires to create change and BE the change in the world.

# MAGIC BULLETS

Listen, success can only come when you clear out the mental chatter. When you learn to trust your inner voice and peel away the layers that are blocking your magnificence from shining. I'm talking about success in your business and success in your LIFE.

To create change in the world, we must first create change in ourselves.

There are no magic bullets. We don't need to chase the ambulances. If someone has an amazing x-step program or a pill that will change everything, walk away.

The question of *'how do I do this?'* is boring...but the question of *'why am I not doing this?'* is sexy. That's when we go to the deeper levels within ourselves. That's when we step into our power and take control of our own destinies.

I receive emails all the time about how to manipulate emotion to sell more. It's a widely accepted and used step-by-step technique that sounds terribly supportive and deep. The people sending these emails call this a SPIRITUAL approach.

Get to a client's emotions under their dreams and then provide them with you as a solution. It makes my skin crawl "...making the client come to the conclusion that they need you to guide them through it."

**STOP IT.**

You can shine in ways that are truer to who you are simply by dismissing the idea that your shine has to look like the ideal that has been placed upon us.

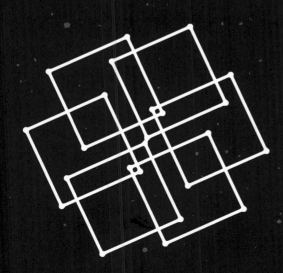

No client needs you.
EVER.

*"They want guaranteed results your coaching program will get them there most effectively."*

## NO.

Don't leverage someone's emotions against them to create a sale.
It's smarmy. It smacks of used cars and swamp land in Florida.

I don't need to leverage pain or hope. I'm not here to promise you more business or self growth.

**You don't need me.**

You may decide you want more support, you may want more learning, you possibly want to be held in a sacred space, AND I'm totally up for that.

*"Bring them back down to where they currently are and show them the pain that they feel right now. How much they really do dislike the situation that they're in, and that it's not good for them to stay there."*

## HELL NO.

I've been sold to that way. It feels horrible. I felt disempowered. I felt small and weak and looked to the other person to help 'save' me, like if I didn't sign up I would be forever stuck. I don't ever want to make another person feel like that. EVER.

I don't want to be treated as someone who needs their emotions to be leveraged so that I can be sold to—and **IF I DON'T WANT TO BE TREATED THAT WAY, WHY WOULD I TREAT OTHERS LIKE THAT?**

Do the techniques work? Absolutely. Done properly you can get your sales-person of the year award capitalizing on people's fears and dreams.

I choose not to.

My Change Agent wants to rewrite all of the techniques, to eliminate all the snazzy one-liner marketing ploys being fed to us. It's time to take a stand for being loving and caring service-oriented humans. Stop using manipulation as a tool to creating anything.

There are other ways. Ways that are more supportive. There are ways to not be formulaic about how you approach other living human beings with real life dreams. There are ways to support and uplift, to be more focused on serving them than selling to them.

*I've built a very successful practice without ever manipulating someone else's soul.*

Rise above this please.
It's possible. **I promise.**

If you desire to be an agent of transformation, then help people transform. Help them CHANGE THEMSELVES. Support their Inner Change Agent so that the stories holding them within their own comfort zone become less and less powerful. Teach them that they have the power within THEM.

Love them.
Hold them.
See them.

Don't shoot them with a magic bullet filled with empty promises.

The glamor wears off...and then the transformation you most wanted to bring forward in the world becomes tainted with misdirection.

## BE A CHANGE AGENT.

Walk the path no one is marketing.
Be different in your business.
Be the one who serves so deeply and lovingly that people never forget their time with you.

Just BE magical.

# YOUR BUSINESS...YOUR RULES

I had a conversation last week with a coach who has been at this game for a couple of years. He has immersed himself in training—not skills training, but marketing training. He's spent thousands of dollars to become an internet marketer in the name of building his coaching business. When we spoke, he kept going in circles, explaining to me how all of this marketing training was helping his SEO, and helping him build his list, and also getting him lots of fans.

So I asked him if he enjoyed the marketing more than he enjoyed coaching.

I asked him if all this busy work was getting him clients.

I asked him what he'd be willing to NOT do any more so that he could do the real work—the work that is about transformation, not broadcasting.

He said he wanted to be coaching, not marketing, but he was so committed to his current path that he could not figure out or see why it wasn't working. All he knew was that he wasn't getting clients. BUT if he just tweaked the verbiage on his site a little more, it'd all click.

He was told that this was the way.

He was told that this is the stuff that works.

All I saw was him **SURRENDERING HIS POWER TO OTHER PEOPLE'S FORMULAS.**

I didn't offer him a coaching spot. He isn't ready to be a badass, to write his own rules, and actually do the things necessary for him to create clients. He wasn't ready to be a Change Agent in his own life. He wasn't ready to see other possibilities. He was too enthralled with magic potions and secret systems for success.

## I AM LOOKING FOR...

- people who are ready to write their own rules and create their own path...

- people who are willing to go off trail to find the better vistas...

- people who are willing to dig a little deeper and find the simple answers inside themselves...

## *It's not popular to say that a multi-billion dollar industry has it all wrong.*

AND I'm willing to say it again and again.

# *True change doesn't happen inside a box.*

This is **YOUR** business.

You don't need anyone else to dictate how you create it...unless you do, in which case you might as well be gainfully employed.

If you're not willing to change the rules so that they fully suit you, then you're following the status quo.

Question that.
Your way is your way.
Follow it.

This is your business.

Play by **YOUR** rules.

# CAN YOU CREATE WORLD PEACE, END FAMINE, AND SAVE THE WHALES?

I want to change the world.

I want to create world peace, end famine, and save the whales.

I want to see domestic violence stop across the globe.

I want to never again see someone abused, raped, tortured emotionally or physically, for any reason.

I want to see cancer and disease disappear.

I want every child to have a proper education.

I want to have the resources to help poverty be a thing of the past.

I want to see every person release judgment of others, and help & support & respect & love one another.

## I WANT A LOT OF CHANGE IN THE WORLD.

And it's overwhelming to think that me, an ordinary person, is capable of creating any ONE of those things, let alone all of them.

But I am.
Because I can.

I can help one person expand.

Then that one person helps those around them expand.

And those people help those around THEM expand.

And exponentially my work with ONE becomes a tidal wave of change in the world.

There are no limits to how much one person can accomplish in their lifetime.

I can be the force that helps one person recognize that.

Be the change.
Embody it.
Think big.
Act on it.
Chip away at it.

**Every single person you touch can be the tipping point between the world we know and the world we dream of.**

Ask tricky questions, listen to the answers that show up, and then do what feels really aligned with who you are.

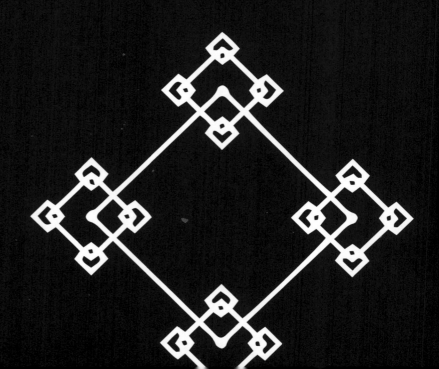

# WHAT'S THE 1%?

Change doesn't have to be a quantum leap.

We don't have to jump off of a cliff.

Change doesn't need to be dramatic and loud and noticeable.

I had a friend who lost 93 pounds.

It didn't happen in a day or a week or a month.

It happened 1 pound at a time.

It wiggled up and down. It plateaued.

She kept at it.

She lost her motivation. She gained it back.

Sometimes she'd starve herself.

Sometimes she'd eat cake for dinner.

Sometimes she'd be super healthy about it.

She kept taking little steps outside of her comfort zone to get the thing she most wanted.

Being a Change Agent in your life means that sometimes you have to do the scary stuff, the stuff that stretches you past your edge between comfort and discomfort. And sometimes it's the tiniest little step, the planting of a seed, choosing water instead of beer with dinner.

Sometimes it's the 1% changes that no one notices, that no one celebrates or shouts about, that make all the difference.

# WORDS CHANGE EVERYTHING

Words can call things in. They can be landing beacons for your dreams and desires.

AND words can keep things away. They can be internal defense mechanisms creating a moat between you and the thing you don't want.

AND sometimes the words you're using to call things in are the very ones keeping them away.

If you don't like saying you coach people, then every time you say you do you send out repulsing energy even though you truly want to coach people.

If you don't like the word *clients* (because your relationship with clients in the past wasn't awesome), then why would you ever want to create clients even though it's the very thing you most want to do.

If you don't like the word *sales* then you will repulse yourself every time it's time for you to perform the act, even though it's the very thing your business needs to succeed.

## USE DIFFERENT WORDS.

Replace *coach* with *guide*. Replace *client* with *sister*. Replace *sales* with *invitation*. Whatever the feel good words are for you...use those. Delete the words that make you contract. Replace them with the words that open your heart and make you expand.

# Words are powerful indicators of what we will receive in life.

Don't TRY to do things. Do them or don't.
Don't say SOME DAY I'll do that. Say I am doing that NOW.

Words are powerful indicators of what we will receive in life.

Change the word, change the vibe...change the results.
Every. Single. Time.

# HANDY DANDY
## *Cheat Sheet*

### REPRESSED & CONSTRICTED CHANGE AGENT

- Resistant to change, Sticks to the status quo

- Fearful of anything outside of my comfort zone

- Apathetic follower, because everyone else knows best and I'll just toe the line

- OR unable to commit to anything other than change, even when the change is harmful or not necessary

- Flaky, non-committal

- Constantly seeking out somewhere other than present place

- Seeks external approval and doesn't take risks that others may not like

- Tries too hard to be different or is outright belligerent

# FOR THE
# CHANGE AGENT & MAVERICK

## FULLY EXPANDED & EXPRESSED CHANGE AGENT

- Grounded and powerful decision maker

- Seeks out change that betters, not as an escape

- Intentional in the type of change sought

- Trusts in oneself and in the Universe

- Doesn't seek approval from outside sources

- Accepts where others are, without judgement, and chooses the path that feels right

- Walks in alignment with self, confidently

- Questions everything, doesn't accept face value and acts in alignment with core values

# LOVER

## — AND —

# BELOVED

Richness of life is brought by giving and receiving love

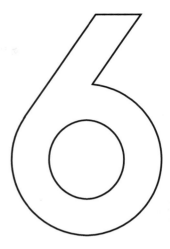

# the sixth seat

Leading from your heart, living life with the connected emotions of love, passion, kindness, understanding—even friendship—is where our Inner Lover stands out.

Love is a two-way street. The Lover knows how to give unconditionally; the Beloved knows how to truly love oneself and to receive unconditionally.

There are no expectations—love is given freely and accepted without question. When I am acting in tandem with the Lover as my guide, there is a wholeness and unity and openness in all things; the total knowing that coming from a place of open-heartedness is the only way to live. From here—from this open-heartedness—it becomes easy to see the divine in all things, even in oneself.

The Beloved demands going within: self-love, self-compassion, and self-acceptance. When we acknowledge all of the flaws, trials, and little imperfections in ourselves, we are able to give and receive more love. It often shows us where we're not being kind to ourselves, and it shows us where we are sitting in judgment of who we are and how we show up.

And this going within—this deep vulnerability—creates a stripping down of pretense so our hearts can be open. There is nothing to hide because love is our greatest protector. We are entangled in a lover's embrace so fierce that even in our nakedness of self, passion overwhelms us until we physically tremble, unaware that our vulnerability is our greatest strength as we lay tangled with our Inner Lover.

*True love, with the Lover and Beloved acting in tandem, is received as much as given.*

The Lover brings passion to our landscapes...

Being passionate about changing the world, about bringing more loving solutions to conflict, about the passion we find in self-care.

This aspect brings our emotions to the forefront...not just love, our Beloved connects us to our deep emotional being.

*This aspect exposes the opening of the heart more and more to the experience of living.*

With the Lover as your guide, there is no thought. There are only feelings of deep connection with all of creation.

When we constrict or deny the lover within, we live a life devoid of passion or deep emotion. We live in fear, behind the emotional walls of protection, afraid to experience heartbreak or disappointment; and in doing so we deprive ourselves of true pleasure, passion, emotion, and love. The divine connection of life itself is essentially cut off at the source—our hearts and our roots. No love going out...

When our Beloved is out of balance we step into comparisonitis and jealousy. Where there is no self-compassion, we take it out on others. We sink into self-loathing, asking what is wrong with us? We become pure wild emotion with no connection to source. Uncontrollable rage, hatred, and abuse all stem from an unbalanced and un-nurtured Lover. No love coming in...

But when we allow the flow of love in and out of our hearts, we learn to love ourselves deeply. We can let that self-love leak out into the world into other people's hearts, and then we find our Lover in the most powerful way. By connecting to the raw vulnerability of true love, we create a life worth living.

# MY BUSINESS LOVER

In my business, the Lover is an important part of my Council. To focus on serving from a deep place of love is paramount. Every word, every coaching session, every sales discussion—it all comes down to me opening up my heart more and more and allowing that passion and love to flow in and out.

The Lover provides the foundation—the cosmic soup—for my business, and it feeds all the other aspects so they can do their part.

*Want to know why inviting someone to work with you is called a proposal?*

> Because at the core it's nothing more (and nothing less) than a beautifully drafted love letter. From your heart to your client's.

If I can lead with my Lover, I can truly see into a person's heart.

That's how I know...

> That's how I know if I want to work with them.
> That's how I can see where I can hold space for them.
> That's how I feel into just how amazing they are at a core level.
> That's how I connect with them in a deeper way.

And once I know, feel, see, and connect, I can tell them. I can tell them from my heart just what I see, just how magnificent they are. I can tell them why I would love to work with them because I've let my Lover take the lead.

There is no catch, no sales pitch.
If my heart knows, then I am honest and I tell them.
There is no expectation of love having to be returned.

Because when my Lover is engaged, while the opening for love to return is totally awesome, there's nothing scary about just giving love.

**That's a worthy proposal.** That's leading with love and respect. Where the client wants to go from there is totally up to him or her. I feel in full integrity that I held nothing back, that I spoke my truth, that I honored the sacred love of being able to coach someone.

# THE HOT GUY

You're sitting at the bar minding your own business and this guy walks up to you and asks for your phone number or worse, just goes straight in and asks to have breakfast with you (it's only 10:00pm...you know what he's referring to). Dude, at this moment you can't even hear his name over the music, and he wants what?

If you're several drinks in, this might sound like a good idea.
It's not.
Check with your friends and move on.

Then another guy comes up. He's got a drink in his hand for you, the same one you were just finishing so you know he took the time to order you what you liked. He tells you he likes your shoes. That's enough to make you want to ask him to breakfast. But hold on...he's not rushing. He asks to sit and you end up spending the next hour or so talking. Talking about who you are and what you want. And when it's time to leave he pulls out his calendar and asks if you're free for dinner sometime next week.

Hell yes you are.
Because he seduced you.

He saw you.
He took the time to get to know you before he took the next step.

So now, I have to ask—who are you showing up as in your business?

*Are you so busy trying to get your clients into bed with you that you're just rushing through the seduction?*

Buy this!
Sign up for this!
Be my Fan!
Get my Newsletter!
Come on...let's go!

Or are you slowing it down?

## TAKE THE TIME TO GET TO KNOW YOUR PEOPLE.

Ask them what their dreams are.
Find out if they like red or white.
Have a real conversation before you do anything else.
Care more about them than you do about you.
Notice their shoes.

Don't rush to get people to become your 'fan'. No one needs numbers—everyone needs CONNECTION. Who are you connecting with in a real way? Don't be in a rush to 'process'—take your time and find the people behind the avatars. Meet—in a real way—the people who rush to hand you their cards.

Be the hot guy who sees you.

# LOVE ON MYSELF A LITTLE

Sometimes I hit a wall. I'm going along and everything is fine. I'm motivated, having fun, things are moving and then—**BAM**—this brick wall with steel reinforcements pops up and I—**SMACK**—walk right into it.

My lucky mojo falls out of my pocket and I lay there on the ground looking around, wondering where the hell I am.

I can feel the bruises.
I feel around to see if anything is broken.
Time to be gentle.
There is no choice.
Close my eyes and rest.
Healing will come.

**Love on myself a little.**

Don't be mad at the wall.
Don't analyze what made the wall.
Don't punch the wall.
Don't break it down in anger.
Laugh a little.
Take a nap.
Put on a bandage.

**Love on myself a little more.**

Allow others to lift me up and brush off the dirt.

Let them love on me a little.

Ask for what I need.

Say it out loud.

Get a hug.

Take a hand.

**Love on myself a little more.**

Don't judge myself for falling.

Don't lose the trust I have in myself to walk

Don't feel less than because I paused.

Don't worry if other people saw me hit it.

**Love on myself a little more.**

Talk about the wall.

Other people have walked into walls too.

It's natural.

It's okay.

Accept the wall.

Thank the wall for giving me the opportunity to allow others in to help and to give myself the time to love on me.

**Love on myself a little more.**

Look up and don't see the wall anymore.

Wonder what happened to the wall while I was sitting there loving on myself.

Get up.

Walk on.

**Love on myself a little more.**

# THE 2 SIDES OF VULNERABILITY

Being fully in tune with our Inner Lover means having a willingness to live without walls built up around our hearts, leaving them vulnerable to the world, naked and seen.

I'm convinced however that there are *two* kinds of vulnerability.

But we all think of just the one...the one that is about our shadows, the things we think others will judge, the things we judge ourselves. It's achingly vulnerable to show up and speak out loud about your flaws, right? So we practice becoming more real, more open with where we are, why and how we struggle.

The beauty of this kind of vulnerability is that when we can express our shame, we diffuse it. We heal ourselves and we give permission for others to heal. Gorgeous right?

But what about the other side of that coin? What about claiming just how magnificent you are? What about shamelessly coming forward and talking about your superpowers, your successes, your triumphs, or of things that come super easy for you?

**That's vulnerability too.**

We get shame. We get sharing our flaws—but if we share our glow then we're no longer accessible, relatable, we will lose friends, family won't understand us anymore, we will come off as too good. We will be judged.

Some of us remember on a cellular level that we will be persecuted, tortured, killed.

The beauty of this kind of vulnerability is that when we can express our light, we magnify it. We align with our highest selves and we give permission for others to do the same. Double gorgeous right?

# *Pay attention...*

## *is it easier to complain or to brag?*

What kind of vulnerability are you willing to dive into, have more of? Both are equally valid in the path of growth.

# THE UPPER LIMIT OF LOVE

How much passion, success, love, joy can you receive before you shut it off?

What are the upper limits of your ability to have love in your life?

Are you worthy of more?
Are you capable of ever returning that love in kind?
There's a sudden feeling of guilt that you'll never
be able to make up for the gift.
There's a need to push it away. Give it back.

Don't compliment me and mean it.
Don't love me more than I love you.

Please put conditions on your love for me so I don't feel I have to live up to
the vastness of that love.

What is your glass ceiling?

Can you ask for help even if you can do it alone?
Can you receive help even when you haven't asked for it?

Opening the petals of your tender heart is so much easier than taking a sledgehammer to its walls

...is what Confucius should have said.

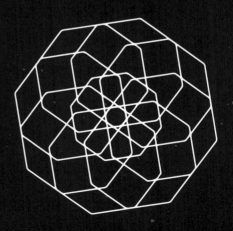

# YOU CAN NEVER GET ENOUGH OF WHAT YOU DON'T REALLY NEED

Love & acceptance comes from you first.

It's a phrase my coach uses often...you can never get enough of what you don't really need.

> You can never get enough love from others because what you really need is to love yourself first.

> You can never get enough acceptance from others because what you really need is to accept yourself first.

You can't get enough from others. Ever. The praise will never be large enough, the applause loud enough, the outpouring of affection, the acclaim, the fame, the approval—your appetite will never be sated until you give it to yourself first.

## *So the question then becomes,*
## WHAT DO YOU REALLY NEED?

> Where do you feel the holes in your power?
> Where are you leaking your awesomeness?

Because we are meant to be whole beings in the world. We are meant to lean into our Inner Council and allow ourselves to love and accept who we are. We can be magnificent creatures of light and dark, fire and ice, pleasure and pain. We are meant to be all of that ourselves, a self-contained little universe of explosive love.

## AND NO ONE ELSE HOLDS THE GLUE THAT KEEPS US TOGETHER.

It's our own personal alchemy of us that is created by our Inner Lover. For when our self love is strong, all the other stories, all the searching for external validation and other people's answers, become inconsequential.

Strengthen our self trust.
Strengthen our self love.
Strengthen OURSELVES.

And allow others to mirror back to us who we are, rather than depending on them to complete us.

# HANDY DANDY
# Cheat Sheet

## REPRESSED + CONSTRICTED LOVER

- Devoid of passion or deep positive emotion, just going through the motions

- Emotional walls of protection, afraid to experience heartbreak or disappointment

- Cut off from love coming in or out, depressed

- Stuck in comparisonitis, jealousy, self loathing and depression

- No self compassion—what is wrong with us?

- Wild emotional responses with no connection to Source

- Uncontrollable rage, hatred, abuse

- Feeling of being all alone in the world

## FOR THE
# LOVER & BELOVED

### FULLY EXPANDED & EXPRESSED LOVER

- Allow the flow of love to go in and out of our hearts

- Build businesses and lives based on passion and service

- Allow the full spectrum of emotions to flow without judgement

- Unafraid of being hurt because of the high levels of self love

- Filled with passion and able to direct it

- Comes from a place of fullness and fulfillment instead of seeking those things

- No judgement of emotions, just allowing whatever is present to come forward

- Never feeling alone

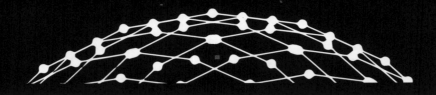

# SEEKER

## — AND —

# KNOWER

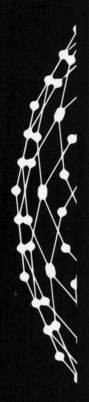

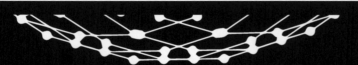

I Question and I Answer therefore I AM

# *the seventh seat*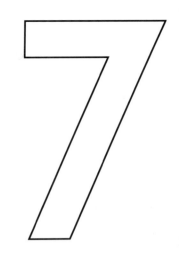

Ah, our Inner Seeker & Knower—its essence is basically the part of us that deeply understands that there are no shortcuts to mastery, only the path and our willingness to walk on it each day.

The Seeker wants to know the questions and the answers and is intent upon reaching higher levels of knowing in all things.

Why are we here?
What is our purpose in life?
I wonder if...?

Those big and little questions all get seen by our Inner Seeker.

Finding the answers to the most existential questions are of course the most expanded way this aspect shows up, overseeing the great libraries of the Universe.

*There are no absolutes, only questions that lead to deeper understanding.*

The undeniable, never-ending search for the next level of expansion. When will it end? Only when the lessons we most need to learn are no longer even in view. So really, never.

The Seeker doesn't search for the absolute, it's the part of us that searches for the next level. That next layer of consciousness that is only gained through both knowing and experiencing. However, the image of a Seeker locked up in the library poring through the books is incorrect, for true expansion comes not from locking yourself away in theory. True growth happens when we apply the knowledge we've gleaned.

It's the part of us that wants to know 'how' and then pursues and experiences whatever answers come up. Every time I hear my clients ask me "how" I have to pause, a silent nod to their own Inner Seeker.

The best part of this quest is that somehow, along the way we've forgotten that we have access to every "how" we ever wanted within ourselves. We just need to lean into our Seeker and suddenly we will receive what we need: the exact person we need to teach us or the book we need to read or the perfect Wikipedia-style answer will appear. My clients may not know exactly the steps to create a radio show, but when they set their Seeker to the task, the steps show themselves. Resources appear at their fingertips.

There's an additional piece of the Seeker that comes into play in the fullest expression of this aspect—the one that few realize is part of a true Seeker—and that's the part that learns experientially, not just theoretically. Merely looking for the next thing to learn isn't all there is...to truly master the knowing of something, one must live it and experience it. I search for the answers and then live in the full expression of my intuition, where the most powerful knowledge is found.

I liken it to being a great scientist. We set up our virtual lab and allow our curiosity to take the reins, without judgment or a preconceived notion of where our research will take us, experimenting with life to test out methods and theories.

The Seeker lives in the 'what if...'; in the 'I wonder...' world. Like a toddler given a bucket of golf balls and a toilet, there's going to be some live action learning happening. It's the part of us that sits with the messages and unlimited knowledge the universe provides and allows the information to flow through and around us. And then the Seeker embodies those truths, allowing the information to leak out into the world, into each action—purposefully becoming new again with each breath of knowledge.

# When our Seeker is unbalanced...

We become un-curious, stubborn, and a bit of a know it all. We pretend we already have all the answers, that we don't need guidance from others (especially our moms, right?), that we know more than most people we meet. We don't need to learn anything else because the rules of life are static and sure. Our way is correct, period.

OR, when unchecked, our Inner Seeker goes into such a constant state of learning that we forget the true nature of the seeker is experiential. It's almost like we have a philosophy degree, content to theorize and pontificate without any action in sight.

These are the times when we read one self help or spiritual book after another, not really changing our lives with the insights, just having insights and moving on to the next book. We start purchasing classes or trying for higher and higher levels of certifications or degrees without actually putting anything into practice. All learning, no action, driven to search for answers without seeing if they are the right ones, which means the search grows more and more desperate and further and further away from what we really want to know...OURSELVES.

# But when we're totally in alignment with our Seeker...

We can't wait to learn more, and we can't wait to try it all out, to see what works and what doesn't. We don't NEED to frantically search for answers outside of ourselves because as we experiment, we satisfy the urge to learn with purpose. That level of knowing becomes something that is just part of approaching our lives and businesses as a grand journey, rather than something to complete.

# THE SEEKER'S GUIDE
# TO THE UNIVERSE

If it's not working it's because, clearly, you don't know enough.

Go get another certification or degree.

Go take another class.

Go buy another book.

Keep searching for the magic missing piece.

Throw spaghetti at the wall.

See if anything sticks.

If after one throw nothing sticks, toss out that spaghetti and buy a different brand.

Because clearly the spaghetti was bad.

Or perhaps we can take a class on how to throw spaghetti better so it sticks on the first try.

Maybe we're just not meant to be spaghetti people.

Try beans.

Other people are doing really well throwing beans.

Give 'em a toss.

And when you're done throwing shit around, pause long enough to watch just how insane the constant need to ask other people "how?" really is, how a true experiment takes more than just one toss or one attempt.

# You can seek forever.

Possibly something will stick.

Or you can stop searching far and wide and look at what you DO have. Re-alchemize what you have. Play with all of the jewels differently. Take what information you already have and pick out the piece that feels really true for you, that feels really good. And then really commit to trying it. Really commit to do it more than once, and tweak it a little each time.

Get to know your path...the one you are creating. AND trust that you know enough.

# TRUTH IS A SPIRITUAL MYTH

The Mayans believed that sacrificing to the Gods was a necessary part of their truth.

The Greeks believed that building giant temples was a way of honoring their truth.

We had shelves of books about different truths in my home growing up. I spent years studying religions and beliefs. I read about Shamans around the world. I read about ancient religions, Western religions, Eastern religions. I studied the bible and mythology. I read about aliens. I learned about crystals and numerology. I studied aromatherapy and listened to mediums. I read about so many different truths I've lost track of them all.

*The search for the 'truth' in spirituality turned up only one thing...it just doesn't matter because truth is a myth.*

What resonated with me didn't always ring true for my Grandmother or Mother. We accepted that. We didn't need to have the same truth. There is no one truth. There is true for me right now. There are things that feel good for me to believe.

It doesn't make the search for truth less valid or exciting, but it makes the search less permanent, a progression of personal puzzle pieces waiting to be put into place.

*For if there is no real truth for everyone, can't we create a personal guide to the galaxy just for ourselves?*

# PRODIGIES WORK TOO

*"Prodigies dazzle us with their virtuoso violin concertos, seemingly prescient chess moves, and vivid paintings...Their performances are hard to explain from a purely deliberate practice perspective. While it's true that many prodigies receive support, resources, and encouragement from parents and coaches early on, such support is typically the result of a demonstrated 'rage to learn.'"*

—excerpt from *Scientific American*

I first became a coach because it felt so natural. I was the one who always gave the powerful insights and advice to others in my life. Coaching was what I was meant to do. I may not have been a prodigy but I'd go so far as to say I had the natural ability to become a great coach...and in many ways I know I was an amazing coach right out of the starting gate.

AND I know now that there's a difference between someone who just goes on natural talent versus someone who takes the time to nurture their abilities.

See, the difference between a naturally good violinist and a prodigy is this demonstrated "rage to learn."

It wasn't enough for me to be a really good coach. I knew that I needed to get to the point in my coaching where I knew without a doubt that if you sat down with me, something in your life would never be the same, some shift would happen that would give you chills.

Becoming a more skillful coach made it easy to build my practice and create abundance.

Mastering my craft allowed me to start charging more and more for those conversations.

And it only happened because I was willing to challenge myself past the edge of my own natural abilities. The prodigies become so because they are driven to know more and do more and immerse themselves in their passion until it fills every piece of their lives. If you've ever seen prodigies in action, they practice and stretch the hell out of themselves each and every day.

They hire teachers and coaches and mentors, they read books or solve problems or sit for hours at the piano, pounding away at songs that can only be learned through repetition and focus.

We are all born talented.
We all have the ability to master anything we choose to.
Is it enough for you to be really good?

# OR DO YOU WANT TO BECOME AN EFFING MAGICIAN?

SHELF HELP:
Those online classes and books we buy to get "better" that we sort of look at and then file away on the virtual shelf only to buy the next one...

STOP IT.

# KNOWING VS. EXPERIENCING

It's one thing to watch and study.
It's entirely different to experience.

I've experienced the shelf-help classes that you listen to once and go 'wow'
and then put them away only to move onto the next.

I've experienced VIP days and retreats and weekend long workshops that
knocked my socks off.

I've experienced being sold to.
I've experienced deep coaching that rocked me to my core.
I've experienced 'meh' coaching.

I've experienced and hired spiritual coaches, business coaches, general
life coaches.

I've been on the receiving end of just about every business model in the
coaching industry.

It is through these experiences that I've built my practice and become the
coach that I am. Many of these have become models for how I refuse to
play. And some are models for my greatest good.

I have never needed a coach (although I have had coaches who made me
feel like I did. I fired them). But I CHOOSE to hire the most powerful coaches

I can because I know that my life's work is to be continually up-leveling ME. I can do it on my own, and I can do it more effectively with a coach.

My first coach cost me $700 for 6 months. At the time I thought it was an outrageous amount of money to invest in someone who was simply there to help me be happier. But there was a calling in my soul, that this was my next level. It was from her that I first felt the siren's song for coaching...that $700 was life changing for me in that one simple insight.

I've hired myself a coach ever since. It's a non-negotiable for me.

When I made that first payment to my last coach Rich, I had a complete panic attack, on the floor crying, wondering how I could spend that much money on something I didn't need. AND I was willing to do what it took to create the funds to make that happen because I KNEW I wanted someone in my corner who would challenge me, who would see me as the magnificent being I am and wouldn't let me forget it, who would hold a space for my higher success.

I am in conversation all of the time with coaches who tell me they can't afford coaching. Perhaps that's true for them...but I couldn't afford ANY of my coaches and I still hired them, each time gaining valuable insights that helped piece together my success.

The most BadAss people I know all have coaches. That's not why they are BadAss—AND I'm sure they'll tell you that it's why they've allowed themselves to show up that way.

# If you're a coach, be coached.

Experience what it's like to cry and laugh and grow while being held by someone powerful. Do what it takes.

# TAPAS FOR THE SOUL

Like tapas for the soul, I have stacks of self development books, some paper and some ebooks, and very few that are finished. Sometimes I judge myself for reading only a few chapters, or a few lines or even just the cover.

And then I pause...is it more important to receive ONE juicy aha or to finish reading the book? Is it okay that I sample the buffet and get a full plate only when it's really, really good?

So I have stacks of books that I have tasted, tiny morsels of deliciousness, like squares of dark chocolate melting on my tongue. And I have a smaller pile...ones that I have devoured, page by page, word by word until I lean back feeling as if I will explode with fullness.

Each have nourished me in their own way, waiting there for seconds when the craving hits...

# SECRET SAUCE

You know all those courses that claim that you can follow steps a-b-c and suddenly you'll make money and be famous and clients will come tumbling out of the sky like manna from heaven?

You're a smart person...do you really, REALLY think it works like that?

Do you really think that next bit of something that someone else has is the secret sauce you've been missing?

It's not.

Know what's missing?
ME NEITHER.
AND I know it's not in that pre-recorded piece of whatever you're thinking of investing in.

Know where it is?
It's inside of you. That missing piece is a part of you, and the crazy thing is... it's not even missing! It's been right there this whole time.

So maybe that class is cheaper. Maybe it's all you think you can afford. Maybe you're craving that little easy button.

But it won't get you to where you really want to go...because that's an inner job. Elevate yourself internally at a soul level and the outer work becomes easier and easier. It's not about learning the latest marketing miracle tool. It's about learning that YOU are the greatest miracle tool.

Think more of yourself than the cheap-ass, mass-produced coursework that people call coaching (that's not coaching—it's an informational product).

Be daring and dream big.
And invest in yourself at a daring, big level.

Why?

Because if it's truly a dream worth going for, then go for it.

Your secret sauce for success lies in the answers you already know. Don't seek the answers outside, invest in finding them **inside**.

# TRUE KNOWING IS...

There are so many different levels of knowing.

There's hearing it and letting it settle into that file marked 'stuff I know.'
There's intimately knowing it intellectually.
There's knowing it in your gut—your gut reaction or instinct.

Then there's really, really knowing it in your whole body as it resonates...

## YES.

I always tell my clients that it doesn't matter to me how many times we need to have the same conversation, say the same things, re-enact the same scenario. It might take one time, it might take 100. But the hope is that the knowledge will sink down further and further each time.

And that at some point there will be this moment where they say 'oh.... **I GET IT** on a whole new level.'

Giving ourselves the opportunity to truly know something means we need to live it, breathe it, BE it. It's no longer some foreign object in our system. It's in us, it is us. True knowing isn't seeking. It just is.

# HANDY DANDY

## Cheat Sheet

### REPRESSED & CONSTRICTED SEEKER

- Un-curious, stubborn, know-it-all

- Unwilling to seek guidance or mentors

- Rules of life are static and unchanging

- Intellectual snobbery

- Never growing

- OR in a constant state of learning without experiencing

- Believing answers indiscriminately, seeking answers without caring if they are the right ones

- Desperately searching for other people's ways instead of your own way

# FOR THE
# SEEKER & KNOWER

## FULLY EXPANDED & EXPRESSED SEEKER

- Curious, beginner's mind in all things

- Happy to glean from the wisdom of others

- Life is a never ending journey of unfoldment

- Everyone has something to teach and learn

- Always expanding

- Balance between book learning and experiential learning

- Choosing to believe knowledge that feels right, not just knowledge that is the easiest to find

- Finding one's own path and answers outweigh the belief that other people know more

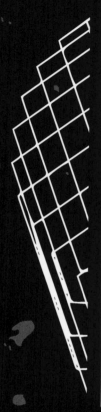

# MANIFESTOR

I am the architect of my own prosperity

# the eighth seat

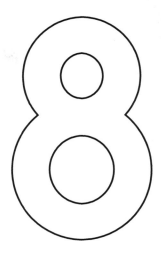

Physical gratification, ahhhhhh. Abundance. SPACE, filled with luxury and human experiences—no timelines, no control, no rushing. Total surrender AND powerful visions. Calling in the vision of greatness. Calling in the magic, and then responding to the nudges. Being present to take action and move forward.

The Manifestor is about that perfect harmony with the earth and the physical plane. It's the part of us who loves to care for our bodies, who will go to a yoga class and drink green smoothies and have magnificent spa days.

It's connected to the soil and the water and the wind.

## THE MANIFESTOR CREATES GOLD AND BEAUTY.

It feels the arousal of passion and the hot tears streaming down our face, smells Grandma's home cooking and the flowers that grow outside of her windows, dances in the rain and wraps us in the embrace of the wind, and sits in harmony.

When the Manifestor takes the lead, we build our homes...we create our business...we run, swim, jump, stretch and care for our bodies as temples... we see the colors all around us.

## WE HAVE PHYSICAL BODIES AND ARE GOVERNED BY THE LAWS OF THIS EARTH.

And yes, we manifest like a badass through this aspect because it understands that the physical plane is ours to play with and to manipulate in countless ways.

This aspect isn't about manifesting Law of Attraction Secret stuff...it is that true embodiment of the words SURRENDER and PRESENCE on the physical plane...A connection with our most profound trust in God, trusting that we have the power to create anything we can imagine, any business, any house, any mate, any friends. There is no separation between the inner world and the outer world. All things are possible—a direct line to unlimited potentiality. This aspect of us is fearless, not because we don't hear the fear, but because we trust the messages from our soul.

It's the connection to the magic all around us if we take the time to breathe deeply and really see it.

## IT'S US AT OUR MOST GROUNDED.

If we're out of balance with our Manifestor, we feel disconnected from our physical body. I remember I used to own a little Honda hatchback in college, and I must have closed that stupid trunk on my head hundreds of times, simply because I wasn't paying enough attention to where my body really was. I was scattered and ungrounded and, evidently, spatially unaware.

When we gain weight or feel our body isn't well, it's usually the Manifestor that needs some extra attention, so we become more aware of ourselves as a temple.

Emotionally, when the Manifestor needs love, we feel mistrustful, filled with victim-like thoughts. We live with a lack mentality, like 'poor me' or 'I'm always broke' or 'fat' or 'old' or something equally unloving to our own humanity.

But when we're really grounded, feeling healthy and vibrant and fully present in the current moment, we know our Manifestor is shining and ready to roll. We experience deep love and connection with ourselves. The unlimited potentiality of abundance and prosperity becomes our new reality.

# FISHING FOR SUCCESS

A boy goes fishing at a nearby creek and comes home empty-handed. He tells his dad there were no fish in that creek.

The next day he walks an hour (think olden times when an unattended child was actually a thing, okay?) to a different creek and comes home empty handed again. No fish in that creek, he tells his dad.

The next day he goes to a creek 3 hours away. Again, no fish in that creek.

Confused, his dad decides to go see for himself and he sees plentiful fish in all 3 creeks. When he gets home he tells his son what he saw and his son says 'but dad I put my hook in the water and it came up empty so if there are fish then surely there's something wrong with my fishing pole'.

See the real difference between a struggling entrepreneur and a successful one is the successful one drops that hook more than once or twice. In truth, they learn to hear no over and over again. If you can seek out the 'no' answers, 'yeses' will actually start coming in.

We cannot manifest success without dipping the hook in again and again and truly believing there are fish.

*To succeed you have to be willing to hear*
*NO more than anyone else.*

Who cares that a couple of days ago you sent invitations that weren't answered? Who cares that no one replied to that offer you posted the other day? Who cares that yesterday that client you really, really wanted told you they don't have the money right now to coach with you? Have you sent more since then? Have you said 'next' and moved onto the next invitation or proposal?

Or did you drop your hook once and then decide that there's something wrong with your hook or your bait or the creek or YOU?

# THE TRUTH ABOUT
# MONEY BLOCKS

There was a time when I thought my money blocks were holding me back from success. I searched out coaches and classes and books about releasing money blocks and creating abundance. I dedicated myself to studying and practicing everything about money because surely that was the reason I was failing. I started working on the blocks—throwing every spiritual tool I could at them. And things did start to change...I started receiving money and clients.

But here's what I realized—that was just a coincidence. Ultimately, at the same time I was working on the blocks, I was also changing how I was doing business. It wasn't the blocks that were holding me back. Now wait just a minute...the blocks are real but stick with me here...

## I WAS AVOIDING ASKING FOR MONEY & SALES.

I was avoiding conversations so I wouldn't have to sell. I covered it all with fancy marketing and clever posts. I appeared to be thriving because I was out making bold offers in the world. But it wasn't working because energetically I didn't really want to have a sales conversation. So when I did they often failed.

Here's what I discovered...**there was a parallel path that didn't have blocks in the road.** There was the path that was sales conversations and asking for money that had a brick wall of resistance—the one that clever coaches are telling you they can help you break down over time. AND there was a path—one step to the right—that led to the same success and didn't involve selling per-se and was miraculously wall-free.

So while the masses stood in front of the trendy money-block wall, I side-stepped.

I walked into the flow of my business.

I stopped selling.

## I STOPPED TRYING TO GET ALL OF THE TIME, AND I STARTED WALKING ON THE PATH OF GIVING.

I rejected all of the sales conversation models being taught to me where I leave people in pain, where I withhold from them, where I cleverly lead them to handing over their money so they can get the rest of the answers.

Instead I just started serving. I started giving away full coaching sessions. I treated a potential client the same way I treat my paid clients—helping them solve issues and have breakthroughs. There was no expectation of a sale, there was no pitch or strategy. And yet my practice filled up. Time and time again, I was giving my gifts and they were paying me back 10—fold.

The fastest path around my supposed money blocks wasn't through, but by finding a different way. My way ended up being a way that didn't feel like sales...a way where money is exchanged enthusiastically and with love.

So do you truly have money blocks? Possibly. Can you still succeed with the blocks in place? Absolutely...just ask: what is your parallel path?

# SHEER DUMB LUCK

"Five points will be awarded to each of you for sheer dumb luck"—and yes I am enough of a Harry Potter fan (geek) to actually have that phrase embedded in my mind. I try for the accent, too, but it never quite sounds the same.

How many of you are operating your business relying on sheer dumb luck? Are you depending on your clients to fall into your lap by chance?

I was talking with one of my coaches the other day and she said to me—"Stacy, in tennis you very rarely get a lucky shot. They happen, but you can't expect to win matches depending solely on the lucky shots. You have to be able to play the game."

The same thing goes for business. You will get some lucky shots—the clients who fall into your lap thrilled to be working with you. And you can't expect to build your business depending on someone to fall from the sky. Listen, I'm a huge fan of manifesting your desires, and I do believe that with the proper mindset we can attract everything we need and want. But there's a secondary step to properly manifesting in your business, and it's called ACTION.

*You have to show the Universe that you are willing to take the actions necessary to make the very thing you are asking for become real.*

You have to be willing to ask people to be your clients. Can you go out on a limb? Can you create the opportunities for the Universe to reward you and support you?

The more matches you play, the more lucky shots you'll get, but you have to be out on the court hitting ball after ball. The most talented players in the world still hit ball after ball to get better. They practice hitting and yes, they practice visualizing themselves winning and becoming one with the ball.

You have to get pissed off enough that you're willing to put the time and practice into learning how to play better so you don't get your butt kicked every time you play.

Either that or quit.

Because you'll never really get anywhere in your business if you show up and wait for miracles.

**5 points for sheer dumb luck doesn't get you very far...**

# MAGIC

Magic isn't something that happens "to" you or "around" you. It's not something you can wait for...Sitting in anticipation for some fairy godmother to come wave her wand.

*If you want magic,*
*you have to be willing*
*to* CREATE *it.*

Dust off your own wand and wave that sparkly stuff all around. It's in YOU.

# SAY NEXT

The difference between the entrepreneurs who charge top dollar and the entrepreneurs who don't is that they are willing to hear NO more than anybody.

It's nothing personal, it's code for '**NEXT**'.

Let's talk about the **HELL NO**. And more importantly the importance of releasing those NOs to make space for your **HELL YES**.

I sent my coach a message...I outlined 3 potential clients I was really excited about. They had visions and purposes that really inspired me and were PERFECT for my upcoming group program. The problem was that each of them said "hell yes, I just need to figure out how to come up with the money". My question truly was, how do I move forward with them? What message can I send them to really get them in action?

His response was frustrating as hell (true to form)...Until the money is in your account, they are not YESes—they are NOs. That in order to create the hell yes I had to create clearer agreements.

After a couple weeks of pouting and letting that sink in, I realized my hand was stuck in a monkey trap. My perfect clients were in that gourd and I grabbed onto the idea of coaching them...and then didn't want to let go. My energy was trapped around converting them instead of opening up and letting them go. I wanted them more than they wanted coaching.

So I opened up my hand and let go.

I acknowledged each of them for what they really were—HELL NOs.

I sent messages along the lines of

> *"Either you're in or you're not. This isn't meant to be a pressure, instead this is meant to take the pressure off of you, because until you hit that Paypal button, you're saying hell no to working with me. And that's okay. This is an investment in yourself you might not be ready for now. But the minute you're ready to make this investment, it's going to come back to you soooo powerfully."*

Free of the entrapments of a "YES BUT..." allowed me to hop back into creation mode. I started filling up my calendar with more interviews, allowing me SPACE to call in the right person.

**Want to hear the best part?** The second I released them, literally ALL 3 signed up, money in the bank.

# *Where are you keeping your hand in the monkey trap?*

What can you release to make space for the magic to happen? It doesn't mean that what you release won't happen, but it does mean that you'll have energy for that or something better...

# PERMISSION TO WANT

The more abundant my life becomes, the more I convince myself that I want very little; that all my needs are fulfilled and that it would be selfish to still desire more.

That I **NEED** less is true. I don't need to fill gaping holes in my consciousness, to make me feel prettier or richer or cooler or more free.

So what's the point of wanting more?

To which I reply, who cares?

# I LOVE
## WANTING AND DESIRING.

Sometimes we deny even the thought of wanting extra. But that's lack and limitation isn't it?

There are no limits to what we can create in this world. Even if we have everything...We can still find something we want.

Even if it's as small as a cupcake (which is always on my list) or as large as a charitable foundation that gifts millions of dollars to repair struggling economies.

The point is that **every creation on the planet starts with a WANT...** A desire powerful enough that someone sets out to create it.

So every couple of months I sit down and write out 100 things that I want. And miracles happen. I've launched businesses and fed my soul from this list. I go back and change a few into 'I am creating' statements. Some I never look at again simply because I wanted them in that moment and not in this one. Some wants aren't important or things I can control or create.

That's okay. It's about allowing myself to simply dream.

And dreams can change the world.

*Can you allow your desires to be spoken into the world without shame or guilt?*

Experiment. Get to 100.

**SEE WHAT CHANGES...**

Be less concerned with building a spiritual business and more aware of building your business **spiritually**.

# THE VOID

Do you honor your natural flow state?

Being an entrepreneur is cyclical. Let's face it, we feel invincible one day and think we suck the next (okay sometimes it happens in minutes instead of days...).

So what happens in the void when our flow is ebbing?

We get FOMO (Fear of Missing Out) and we get into comparisonitis. We feel impatient and channel our inner Veruca Salt (I want it NOW). And we feel like we must be doing something wrong.

Hear this...

*What you do with the void is the differentiator between those who are succeeding and those who are not.*

You can fight it. You can go down kicking and screaming.

You can start creating anything to get you out.

You can start throwing spaghetti at the walls in the slim hope that something will stick.

You can start yelling at the seeds you've planted to 'GROW DAMMIT'.

You can start looking outside of yourself for results to prove that you're not as incompetent or (insert your own not-so-loving word here) as you think you are.

You can chin up and force your way to the other side, push through.

And none of that is a long term solution.

Because tomorrow, next month, whenever, you'll have to do it all over again. And eventually, all that fighting leads nowhere but where you are now.

**OR...**

You can surrender.

You can recognize this as part of the process.

You can realize that all seeds grow in their own time and you can relax.

You can believe that you've done your part and you can use the ebb to reflect on what you really want to be creating, you can use the space to clear the path for further growth.

You can be gentle with yourself and enjoy the break.

You can learn to TRUST YOURSELF, and the Universe-Source-God. All good things are on their way because you've done your part.

You can learn to float.

## THE EBB WILL HAPPEN AGAIN.

AND if you've strengthened your own internal trust muscles, then you know you will be safe and you will continue to grow each time it does. No fighting frenzy. And eventually you will float back into flow, easily and seamlessly.

The true difference between those who are truly succeeding and those who aren't all comes down to trust.

Ask yourself,

## *"Where do I need to trust myself, my process and my flow more?"*

# HANDY DANDY
# Cheat Sheet

## REPRESSED & CONSTRICTED MANIFESTOR

- Disconnected from physical body

- Ungrounded, spatially unaware, head in clouds

- Prone to substance abuse or other ways of not being on this earthly plane

- Feels unwell often

- 'Lack' mentality

- OR No spiritual connection because overly earthbound, can't see past human existence

- No luck, nothing works out, cursed

- Struggles with life

# FOR THE
# MANIFESTOR

## FULLY EXPANDED & EXPRESSED MANIFESTOR

- Fully aware of own physical and spiritual presence

- Grounded

- Healthy feeling

- Abundance mentality

- Giving body and spirit the substances that fuel it

- Beautiful balance between human experience and connection with Source

- Lucky in life, things magically work out, blessed, trusting

- Life is easy

# SAGE

If Buddha, Ghandi and Jesus walked into a bar...

# *the ninth seat*

This aspect is the yummy, juicy, completely spiritual woowoo side of who we are. It's the part of us who meditates, who is in constant communication with our highest self, and who is, in fact, the voice of our highest self as it merges with source.

This is the part that believes without a shadow of a doubt that there is nothing wrong with us.

We don't have some mysterious blocks to success.

We're not doing anything wrong.

We're not incapable or unworthy or any of those other things we sometimes say to ourselves.

When we see ourselves from the aspect of the Sage, we see someone who knows enough and is enough to create the biggest vision we can imagine.

We see someone who is powerful and magical and awesome.

We see someone thoroughly worthy and capable.

The Sage takes our hand and asks that WE see the possibilities of our existence.

# EXPLORE.
# EXPERIMENT.
# CREATE.
# **DREAM.**

The Sage is our courage and our heart. This aspect holds sacred space for us.

For it KNOWS that **WE ARE ENOUGH.**

It has lived lifetimes knowing us, learning the curves of our consciousness, being intimate with our heart's desires, holding the deep well of our soul... waiting and nudging it into the world—one shiny piece at a time.

Nothing to fear.

For it has seen it all and knows it all and believes in US.

The Sage isn't just wise, it's beyond wise...so connected to the juiciness of our soul that there really is no separation between where we end and where spirit begins. Long has been this aspect's journey as it pulls from the wisdom of the ages. The Sage can tell us each and every story, weaving each one for our highest purpose.

The Sage contains the duality of us...

Light and Dark.
Heaven and Earth.
Yin and Yang.
Fire and Ice.

For in the space between our contrasting selves lies true wisdom and balance. There is space for both in each of us, for the shadows and for the divine, for being grounded in the soil and elevated to the heavens, for feeling fire and passion of desire and the overwhelming coolness of simply knowing. The Sage knows when it is time for calling in any of these aspects to the table.

*The Sage is the truest self, the one who knows our purpose and mission, the one who has the visions of all possible futures.*

# YOUR DIVINE LETTER

*"Do you know what you are? You are a manuscript of a divine letter. You are a mirror reflecting a noble face. This universe is not outside of you. Look inside yourself; everything that you want, you are already that."*

—Rumi

Your life, your business. You are paving your own destiny. There are those who seek to tell you that if you do x-y-z your life will change, success will be found. They are false prophets. Those of us who have the heart of a warrior know that the battle is not what is seen on the outside. Those seeking to read that divine letter we have written on the pages of our being understand that our outer success is a reflection of our inner world.

If you have chaos inside, so shall it be outside.

If you have doubt inside, it will manifest without.

If you are constantly up-leveling your inner world, your outer world will also up-level.

## YOUR SUCCESS ISN'T FOUND IN A TO-DO LIST.

It's found when you really truly learn to trust your internal guidance system.

" Be a lamp, or a lifeboat, or a ladder. Help someone's soul heal. Walk out of your house like a shepherd."

—Rumi

Are there external things you need to do to succeed? Absolutely. Those can be learned, especially when you have a teacher who helps you anchor them in your core, not just in your head space.

And with a well paved inner world, stepping into those things is easy. It feels right instead of hard.

That's where we play. We can create from the inside out, building brilliance, casting aside the stories we've been holding onto; for your success, you are already capable of brilliance and succeeding at high levels. We just need to polish off those mirrors and start afresh.

Are you ready?

# HOW INTUITIVE ARE YOU?

Most of the coaches—hell, pretty much all of the coaches—that I speak with will own up to the fact that they are intuitive people. That they coach intuitively and they're really good at that. And that's great. When I first started coaching I told everyone that they were going to be receiving intuitive coaching, that they were hiring an intuitive coach.

And here's where I went astray...

1. **I didn't consciously work on my own intuitive skills, I just leaned into them enough to have a good coaching call and then went about my life.** My intuition lived in the vacuum of my coaching space. I didn't stretch my intuition. I didn't train my intuition.

   I learned slowly over time to trust my nudges. Once I really started focusing on being as badass intuitive as I could possibly be, my sessions went from really good to holy cow. Intuition is like a muscle. I needed to develop it and work it out and learn to really, really have confidence and trust in it.

   It is a natural skill that I forgot to nurture to it's fullest potential.

2. **I didn't let my intuition lead my business.** I didn't trust it. Intuition was fine in my coaching calls, but business was serious brain stuff. That was a hard skill to learn, to surrender when you know you have a to-do list. AND the more I surrendered the easier things flowed and the more money and abundance I created in my business and life.

I also didn't understand that running my business intuitively is a very active and CREATIVE process. And it doesn't look like what anyone is teaching. That was exciting and also a struggle for me...to fully abandon all the ways I had learned over the years and trust that my way was not only okay, but was the ONLY path to my own success.

I had to develop my skills as an intuitive to be a better intuitive coach.

I had to incorporate intuition into ALL parts of my life, not just the coaching space.

I had to seriously trust that I hadn't gone completely loco in the process.

Abandon all of your carefully crafted marketing or outreach plans.
Divorce yourself from the 'shoulds'.
Lean FULLY into your intuition.

# GET YOUR TRUTH AND BE POWERFUL

I witness clients every day who come to me not understanding just how powerful they really are. I witness the beauty and power of someone aligning with who they are at a deep level. I experience it personally every day.

AND that doesn't mean we are free of fear or doubt, it doesn't mean that our humanness never shows up. It does show up...everyday. And I hope it always does to some extent, because those times are great indicators that I'm moving forward to the next level of consciousness for myself. Those are moments when I KNOW I'm pushing the edge of my comfort zone and it's time to keep moving. To allow it to flow through me, to recognize how powerful those moments of intense energy are.

I can only speak to what is true for me.

I stand up and take a stand for whatever it is I believe in, but I never expect others to believe or follow. I hope what I say or write resonates with some, that tiny shifts happen. But I don't TRY to make change anywhere—because that's not up to me.

I don't preach.
I'm not a guru.
I don't have all of my shit together.
I just try to show up as the best version of me I can be in this moment.

Who would I need to be to always be powerful? To come from my truth in all things? To shed the internal judgments of myself and allow the messy, unruly me come through?

I've been trying to 'figure it out' and 'compartmentalize it'. I've been trying to define it, understand it, express it. We can change that in an instant. Today, we can feel it...how far we can push our inner limits, cross those invisible lines that say everything past this point is impossible.

We don't need to define my power.
We don't need to judge it.
We don't need to force it out.
We don't need to fight with it for control.
We don't need to see it as a threat.
We don't need to feel like it is something outside of me, separate and different.

I just need to allow it to permeate my heart, to breathe it in and out. To experience it as the true me, the one waiting to be seen.

# *I just need to BE.*

# THE LOOK OF SPIRITUALITY

There's a look and a language attached to being spiritual.

There's an expectation that you'll be all serene and upper-chakra-ey.

There's this idea that material earthly things aren't the real goal.

That money is the opposite of spiritual.

That love is always pure.

That meditating means silence and sitting and OM-ing.

That being truly spiritual is a sterile experience, free of all ego and mind and judgment and that a spiritual lifestyle is clean and clear of all frustrations.

That somehow the ultimate end result is that we expand past all expectations of what it means to be human.

And it all kind of misses the mark for me.

I AM human.

I look the way I look...and what if a kick-ass pair of heels makes me channel my inner self even MORE powerfully? I love wearing designer jeans and carrying premium handbags. Kate Spade is a badass.

I like engaging all of my chakras...and my hands and my brain and my whole body.

I refuse to live in la-la crown chakra land when there's a cheesy pop song waiting to be sung at full throttle in the car; or a friend sitting with me on the couch laughing hysterically at some stupid joke, glass of wine in hand.

I eat chocolate. Not the wholesome pure good-for-you kind of chocolate but the 'makes you weak in the knees like great sex' kind of chocolate, rich and decadent and luxurious.

I love all of the experiences that money buys. I love that I can help others. I love that I can complete my mission. I love that I can take a trip or a class or whatever just because.

I am not a good 'meditator'. My body wiggles. My butt falls asleep. My most profound moments of growth are when I connect by writing. Meditation just isn't my tool.

# My ego is my greatest teacher. I have no wish to silence her.

Things frustrate me...the stupid driver on the road who cuts me off—yeah, he pisses me off. Doesn't make me a bad person, just makes me human with real human emotions. Can I get over it? Of course, instantly. But unless I find myself in a bubble, frustrations are just a part of our experiences.

# BEING SPIRITUAL FOR ME IS **MESSY**.

Me as a spiritual being changes every day in every situation. I will not be labeled. I will not be all love and light and glitter coated rainbows simply to be known as some spiritual icon.

Light and dark.
Ebb and flow.
High and low.
Yin and yang.

Spiritual for me is all of that. It's experiencing nature and being thoroughly metropolitan. It's feeling all of my emotions and allowing them ALL, whether they are deemed part of my highest purpose or not. I am an empath so I'll feel them all anyhow, from me and from others...might as well live them to their fullest expression.

Perhaps this makes me 'less' spiritual or evolved or aware. But I went that route already and it felt more like a role than real life. When I found myself, what I found behind the guru-speak was a beautiful human experience laid out before me, waiting to be really lived.

For this part of me who embraces all of my humanity I rely on my own Inner Council to guide me, inspire me, help me expand.

# SURRENDER ISN'T
# A NASTY WORD

It sounds so passive right? Surrender. I'll never forget the moment one of my clients came to a session and announced "Stacy, I've decided to surrender my business to God," and I thought well shit, now we have some real work to do!

Because surrender is the most active way to live.
It's counterintuitive.

My son plays Rugby. In rugby you're taught to carry the ball and run INTO the tackle. It isn't instinctual. It's a trained move. Because let's face it, very few people really want to run into that guy wanting to bring you down. We want to avoid the tackle. We want to run around and past him. That guy's scary. So our survival instincts kick-in.

My son also plays football where he's taught to avoid the tackle at all costs. He's been trained for years to avoid the tackle or to help others to avoid the tackle so the ball carrier doesn't get stopped or hurt.

But that's not so in Rugby. Everything he's been taught no longer applies. Every survival skill he has no longer serves him.

To avoid injury and to play the game, he has to do the opposite and run into the tackle.

He has to surrender it all to effectively play the game.

People aren't trained to run a business using their hearts instead of their heads. People who surrender won't do things that look like business building during business hours. They'll meditate or read. They will nurture their spirits and bodies. They will write when inspiration hits and they will ask for the inspiration to be badass.

They will not be on the path that everyone else is on.
Everything they've been taught no longer applies.
And that's scary.

It takes constant monitoring to make it work.

Question every action—is this in alignment?
Question every decision—is this in alignment?
Question every thought—is this in alignment?

You think surrender is turning over and giving up?
Nothing could be further from the truth.
Surrendering is running straight into the tackle.

## IT IS THE PATH OF A TRUE WARRIOR.

# I SUCK AT MEDITATING

5 minutes into class I've already gone really deep, really fast. I've had my insight, I feel grounded and balanced and refreshed and inspired.

I'm done.

Everyone else is just settling into it.
Okay, 5 minutes is wrong.
I'll try again.
I try listening to the teacher.
Her voice just annoys me. She's talking about someplace I don't want to go, and why the hell would I want to take a swim in a lake? I don't know what's in that lake!

Wrong again. Try again.
Breathe.
Put hands on ears so I don't follow the swimmers. I'd rather go sit on the beach in Hawaii. Let's go there.
I hear the voice telling me to relax my hands.
Dammit.

Now my hands can't stop dancing. They sway and drift, playing with the energy being created in the room like cosmic play-doh. I notice the person 2 seats over has some darkness in her body. I toss some play-doh her way.

The person next to me puts her hand on my leg to get me to stop moving so she can om.

Dammit.

So I curl up into a ball. Hands over eyes—it's so bright in that freaking room. That candle might as well be a lighthouse. My thumbs drift into my ears. Ah, no more voice droning on about a garden. I can now listen to the voices of my soul who want to hang out and chat some more.

Solitude comes to me in the form of a hunched over, knees pulled to chest, face covered, ears plugged, in a completely not zen sort of way.

I suck at this.

I sat down with my spiritual coach and I let her know what a bad mentee I was. I confessed that I am a spiritual fraud incapable of om-ing with the best of them.

I thought she would fire me as a client for sure.

Instead she laughs at me.

'What makes you think that because you do it differently, it is any less valid? What makes a good meditation? Some people walk, or eat. Some people are silent for a week while living their normal life. And some people sit cross legged with hands gracefully placed upwards on their knees for hours at a time.

A good meditation is being able to connect with the real you and with Spirit. That's it.

You have everything you need in moments. How lucky is that? It doesn't matter what position you sit in because you can do it anywhere sitting any way you want, even squinched up in a ball. You don't even have to have a guide to take you deep. And you have dialogues with your guides without having to even om-it-out. So why do you need to feel like you suck when actually, you just do it differently?'

**In that moment, all the shame I'd held onto for my spiritual connection looking different from the standard path was released.**

I may suck at sitting still.

But I don't suck at meditating, even if from the outside it may appear that I do.

The root of who you are,
the core of who you are,
isn't perfect.

It's the flaws and
imperfections of our souls
that make the spiritual
journey an adventure.

# THE SAGE OR YOUR EGO

Our Sage KNOWS.
Our Ego thinks.

Our Sage has no need to define.
Our Ego cannot operate without definition.

Our Sage is whole.
Our Ego is compartmentalized.

Our Sage doesn't attach itself to stories.
Our Ego creates and lives by the stories.

We can live with both.
We are in fact the bridge between the two, aligning our highest spiritual selves with simply being human.

This isn't a war we need to wage.
This is a marriage of opposites.
Neither is right or wrong, just different.

We get to choose who plays in every situation.
We get to choose what tools we want to use.
We get to choose to be in council with both at any given time.

# HANDY DANDY
# Cheat Sheet

### REPRESSED & CONSTRICTED SAGE

- Imbalanced and empty

- Prophetic to the point of crazy, standing on a corner with end of the world signs

- Locks up intuition in Pandora's box

- Believes that spirituality has rules and those not following them are condemned

- Judges those outside of their faith as immoral and campaigns to save them

- Becomes committed to only the mind, science, physical proof

- Wanders lost, without purpose or mission or curiosity to find either

- Lives in darkness and shadow

# FOR THE **SAGE**

## **FULLY EXPANDED & EXPRESSED** SAGE

- Fulfilled internally

- Allows the voice of God to flow through them

- Intuition is a powerful muscle played with in all areas

- Faith is like breathing, no rules, just allowing it to be a part of all actions and breath

- No judgement of others for where they are in their lives or for their beliefs, coming from a place of curiosity and love

- Understands that laws of physics and Spirit are intertwined

- Trusts own purpose and mission and is living into it each day

- Filled with joy and light

# THE
# TENTH
# SEAT

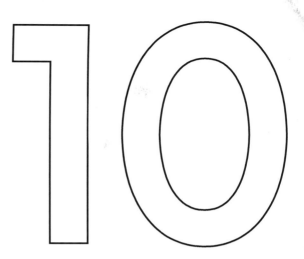

I used to have this image of the NINE as UNAT-
TAINABLE SPIRITUAL ICONS OF PERFECTION.

BORING!

Can you imagine going through life with a bunch
of pontificating gurus prattling in your ear?

What about the realness and rawness of simply
being human? Can you imagine that?

The Council is totally not perfect.
It is simply me.

Here's the deal... our Inner Council at its best is
a symphony of all the greatest parts of who we
are and who we can be. When each is in balance,

or even better, in full expansion, we become powerful and our inner world explodes only to manifest into our outer world — our business, our relationships, our things...our world.

When we sit *with* our Inner Council — when we occupy the 10th seat — we sit with the awesomest parts of ourselves.

I don't know what it will look like for you to communicate with Your Council. What I DO know is that your life can take on a different path if you really start talking to each member on Your Council, taking the advice and nudges from your own inner voices.

## *Your life could exponentially explode.*

Ask yourself, where are you questioning?
Where do you need support or counsel?
Where are you unsure?
Where are you stuck?

Then allow yourself to lean in and listen because Your Council is just waiting for you to ask.

By having meetings with each of our advisors, we get the full scope of what we need to do to expand. And, this expansion can be into anything we want to create in the world.

## HOW DO WE START WORKING WITH OUR COUNCIL?

By really knowing who makes up the Council. By allowing their voices to inform you of what they need.

This is as simple as having a conversation with yourself.

For me, sometimes I draw a map asking each one in turn — *what do you need right now?*

Sometimes it's a meditation and a dialogue.
Sometimes I take a breath and one voice responds clearly.

Set a sacred stage and ask the question that is burning within you...this is a board meeting with yourself. Growing your business, creating a life partner, deciding to study with a specific shaman...whatever it is that you are driven to create in your life, take a moment and feel into it.

> *Is everyone on board?*
> *Who feels constricted?*
> *What does each aspect really need to move forward?*

If you're willing to have the conversation, Your Council is willing to participate. Nothing complicated. No big rituals. Just you asking yourself the questions and then listening for the answers.

# *Take the time to really get to know the character of each aspect within you.*

As you read through this book and began to identify and know each member of Your Council, I am sure you recognized yourself or your situation in some of the stories. Feel into how the ideas and concepts behind the stories and each aspect presents itself in your life. Zoom in on a particular project you're creating and find out what each aspect needs to fully create and complete that project.

Ask one at a time.
Go around the circle.

This book for me is a great example of how I use my own Inner Council. See, after a year of writing, I got stuck.

So I asked my **Creator**, "What is going on with this book? Why aren't we completing it?"

> "... *because it got down to the details and the finishing. That stuff bores me. I have all this time and space to play in, and I plan on putting exciting things first.*"

I asked my **CoCreator**, "What is going on with this book? Why aren't we completing it?"

> *"... because I don't have the platform built yet. I'm afraid that if we don't do that, no one will read it."*

I asked my **Catalyst**, "What is going on with this book? Why aren't we completing it?"

> *"... I love this book. I'm passionate about it. And my flame is low because the fear dampens it. I don't know if I have permission to be excited about it yet."*

I asked my **Leader**, "What is going on with this book? Why aren't we completing it?"

> *"... I don't know! It's frustrating the hell out of me. I'm so tired of this project draining our resources. It's hanging over our heads dangling possibility and all I want to do is finish it, but everyone's fears keep getting in our way. How can I project manage this when not everyone is on board?"*

I asked my **Change Agent**, "What is going on with this book? Why aren't we completing it?"

> *"... I'm with the Leader. You obviously don't want the change that this book will bring into your life or into the lives of others. You must like being an author of 16 UNPUBLISHED books. It keeps us still. I'm not a fan of being still."*

I asked my **Lover**, "What is going on with this book? Why aren't we completing it?"

> "... I'm afraid that I am pouring my heart into this, I'm afraid of how vulnerable I feel and I'm afraid that if we release it I will be sad and alone and will never receive the love back."

I asked my **Seeker**, "What is going on with this book? Why aren't we completing it?"

> "... We don't know how to publish a book. How will you know when it's finished? We should do some more research."

I asked my **Manifestor**, "What is going on with this book? Why aren't we completing it?"

> "... It's never going to look the way you envision it. The physical product is going to be dramatically different and that scares me. I'm scared of being disappointed."

And then I asked my **Sage**. "What is going on with this book? Why aren't we completing it?"

> "... If you publish this I'll be exposed. You've worked a long time to hide me — are you sure we're ready for this?"

Through this dialogue, by breaking it down piece by piece, I realized that my fears were small and not real. The pain I was feeling by holding back, however, that was big. My Catalyst wants to publish, my Leader wants to finish and my Change Agent needs the change. Their counsel made the other's limitation insignificant. I had to trust those parts of me that were READY to support those that weren't.

*So by sitting with each and really hearing where they were, it allowed me to hear the stories and listen to what was most important.*

It's so fun to see how the aspects all work in harmony and inform each other of what we really need. Take for instance those times when we get stuck in creating something...

Not only does our Creator need a little boost, but if we dive in, we'll also see that perhaps our Catalyst isn't really sure what part of the proposed creation to get excited about. Clarity is required.

And, our Lover is scared of the creation being rejected after pouring love into it so we need some extra reassurance.

Our Leader is tired of hanging on to an incomplete project, so we need to create boundaries, and so on.

Working with Your Council can be as simple as allowing each to chime in so that you can make informed choices.

These 10 seats are created by you for you. They are comfortable and fit just right. Their sole purpose is to help you as a whole expand into the world in the most beautiful ways.

## *This book, ultimately, is merely an opening.*

**It's not meant to be a manual or to give you step-by-step, how-to instructions.**

Its purpose is to help you open the dialogue with your own Inner Council.

They're all there, patiently waiting in their chairs for you to witness their voices and see their love for you as you sit in the 10th seat.

# CONVERSATION STARTERS:

*Exercises to start talking with your Inner Council*

These worksheets are also available as a printable download at www.YourInnerCouncil.com

## STEP ONE: WHAT DO YOU WANT?

Allow yourself a moment to wallow in your desires because no journey can begin without them.

Unless the conversation with your Inner Council is "what do I want?" (which is a great conversation, by the way) the most profound place to start is to be clear about what you want to create.

I use this exercise all of the time with my clients. This is a place to dream, to let loose those desires you never speak of, to imagine it all. No wish is too small or too large. Usually there are 2 things that make my list every time I create it — a cupcake & world peace.

Give yourself 15 minutes or so to list 50 things you want.
Try to get specific.
Don't edit.
Don't judge.

Don't stop until you reach 50. If you run out of things before 50, still don't stop. Keep going. Some of my most amazeballs dreams came out 6 numbers past where I wanted to quit.

| | |
|---|---|
| **1** | 11 |
| 2 | **12** |
| **3** | 13 |
| 4 | **14** |
| **5** | 15 |
| 6 | **16** |
| **7** | 17 |
| 8 | **18** |
| **9** | 19 |
| 10 | **20** |

**21**

22

**23**

24

**25**

26

**27**

28

**29**

30

31

**32**

33

**34**

35

**36**

37

**38**

39

**40**

41

**42**

43

**44**

45

**46**

47

**48**

49

**50**

## NOW, PICK ONE TO PLAY WITH HERE...

Make it even more specific, give it the details that allow you to see it, feel it, hear it, touch it. Play until it feels like a real thing you can create.

# I AM CREATING...

## STEP 2: THE CONVERSATIONS

Settle in to ask some questions of each of your Advisors. They have information that will come out as you talk. Sometimes you don't need to talk with everyone (the 4th question will help you with that). Sometimes everyone's input is nice. I like going through the whole panel just in case there is something there that I'm avoiding. Pay attention to the themes popping up in the replies.

AND make up your own questions. Get curious. If the answer doesn't make sense, ask again. If the question doesn't feel right, ask a different one. This is a sounding board, a place to start. Get creative here and have an actual dialogue. See what comes up.

Have fun diving in.

# SIT WITH YOUR **CREATOR**

How would it feel to start or create this?

What doubts do you have that will distract me from creating this?

What do you need to start this?

Which other Council members do you need help from next?

# SIT WITH YOUR **CO-CREATOR**

Who do you need support from?

What doubts do you have that will distract me from creating this?

What do you need to start this?

Which other Council members do you need help from next?

# SIT WITH YOUR **ENROLLER**

What do I need to feel passionate about creating this?

Who do I need to be to get others excited about this?

What doubts do you have that will distract me from creating this?

Which other Council members do you need help from next?

Who do I have to be to lead this to fruition?

What part of this project feels misaligned, needs more organization or more structure?

What do you need to start this?

Which other Council members do you need help from next?

# SIT WITH YOUR **CHANGE MAKER**

What needs to change in me or in the world around me to do this?

What part of this is outside of my comfort zone?

What will make the change feel safer?

Which other Council members do you need help from next?

How can I give myself love and self-care in order to create this?

Where does my heart feel out of alignment with this project?

What do you need to start this?

Which other Council members do you need help from next?

# SIT WITH YOUR **SEEKER**

What do I need to know more about to proceed?

What knowledge do I already have that I can experiment with here?

What doubts do you have that will distract me from creating this?

Which other Council members do you need help from next?

Am I crystal clear with my desire?

Are there any energetic holdbacks, places where I doubt that this will happen?

Do I know how I want this to feel?

Which other Council members do you need help from next?

# SIT WITH YOUR **SAGE**

What spiritual lesson will I need to learn to be able to best create this?

Who will I be once this is created?

What doubts do you have that will distract me from creating this?

Which other Council members do you need help from next?

## STEP 3: START

Now take a moment and really feel into the information you just gleaned from your conversations.

# WHAT STANDS OUT FOR YOU?

A couple of needs will jump out as the places to start.

A couple of blocks will jump out as just stories of no significance, easy to get past.

When everything is out on the table it becomes pretty apparent where to start or what needs more love, time and understanding.

# WHERE WILL YOU START?

Wherever it is, now is the time to start experiencing and stop talking. Your Council is here all of the time at every single step. Talk to them anytime the need in you arises.

To print these questions as a downloadable workbook or to keep in touch and stay posted for updates, classes and other awesomeness, go to **www.YourInnerCouncil.com**

## ALSO BY

*Stacy Nelson*

## Unconventional Wisdom:
*Stories Beyond The Mind To Awaken The Heart*

This book is about nothing in particular. Yet, it's about everything, too. Authentic happiness. Unconventional success. Personal growth in business and life. Effortless living. Courage. Vulnerability. Power. Relationships. Transformation. Being YOU. Inside these pages we guarantee at least ONE insight that will change everything, one ah-ha moment that, if you allow it to settle into your soul, will change you, how you look at your world and how you create your life. We know this to be a fact because it's what we do. We change lives every single day. These are our stories, our lessons, our ideas, our thoughts, our soul ponderings. We don't run our businesses or lives like everyone else. We are unconventional in who we are because we set out to be more and more of who we are meant to be rather than who the world expects us to be. We suspect you're like that too. Dive in and explore and find your own Unconventional Wisdom.

www.UnconventionalWisdomBook.com

## STACY NELSON

is a best-selling Author, Publisher, Coach, Mentor, Jewelry Maker, Multi-Passionista & whatever else she feels like being on any given day, like writing this book in your hands right now.

Stacy helps people throw out all the formulas they've been taught, eliminate the shoulds and smart strategies and even the way business is supposed to look.

She grants her fellow intuitives & empaths a golden ticket of permission to tap IN. Build your business from your heart space. What feels really right? What does that illogical inner voice tell you to do or to be today? Throw out your packages and your 5 steps to selling more anything and relax. What ONE thing do you feel most compelled to do? Create your own systems and containers with your energy. Build the ones that have your unique spiritual signature. Infuse your business with soul.

Please check out her other books and general awesomeness online at...

www.StacyNelsonUnlimited.com

DOWNLOAD THE

# COMPANION
# WORKBOOK

FOR FREE AT

www.YourInnerCouncil.com

13402666R00143

Printed in Great Britain
by Amazon.co.uk, Ltd.,
Marston Gate.